WHAT IS CHRISTIANITY?

BENEDICT XVI

WHAT IS CHRISTIANITY?

The Last Writings

Edited by
Elio Guerriero and Georg Gänswein

Translated by Michael J. Miller

IGNATIUS PRESS   SAN FRANCISCO

Original Italian edition:
Che cos'è il cristianesimo. Quasi un testamento spirituale
Italian translation by Pierluca Azzaro and Elio Guerriero
© 2023 Mondadori Libri S.p.A., Milan, Italy

The translation of this work was funded by the Centro per il
Libro e la Lettura, part of the Italian Ministero della Cultura.

Cover based on the original Italian edition by Nadia Morelli

CONTENTS

Chapter Four

TOPICS FROM DOGMATIC THEOLOGY

Chapter Five

TOPICS FROM MORAL THEOLOGY

Chapter Six

OCCASIONAL SPEECHES AND ESSAYS

FOREWORD

by Elio Guerriero

In 2019 I edited a volume entitled *Ebrei e cristiani*[1] in which I made available to Italian readers the article by Pope Benedict "Grace and Vocation without Remorse: Comments on the Treatise *De Iudaeis*", followed by an exchange of letters between the Chief Rabbi of Vienna Arie Folger and the pope emeritus. Curiously enough, the article by Ratzinger, which was described by some Catholic theologians in the German-speaking world as hazardous to the Jewish-Christian dialogue, was defended by the chief rabbi of Vienna and by other Jewish representatives, both Italian and foreign.

The publication had a good outcome for the dialogue: at the presentation of the book at the Lateran University in Rome, Arie Folger, Riccardo Di Segni (chief rabbi of Rome), and Renzo Gattegna (past president of the Union of Italian-Jewish Communities) were in attendance. Another positive result was the circulation of the book in Italy; moreover, there were other foreign editions.

Encouraged by this precedent, when I met with the pope emeritus to tell him about all these events, I dared to ask him: "Why not gather together all the texts that you wrote in the years following your resignation and publish them as a single volume?" In keeping with a habit long

[1] Benedetto XVI with Rabbi Arie Folger, *Ebrei e cristiani*, ed. Elio Guerriero (Cinisello Balsamo: San Paolo, 2019).

familiar to me, Pope Benedict replied that he would think about it. I later learned that he had started collecting the material, and this was undoubtedly a positive sign.

The situation was complicated by the publication of a volume by Robert Cardinal Sarah, *From the Depths of Our Hearts*,[2] which featured an article by Pope Benedict on the Catholic priesthood. According to some unfriendly [*malevoli*] commentators, among whom German-language authors once again distinguished themselves, the book seemed to be a disavowal of the Synod of Bishops for the Pan-Amazon Region that had been held in October 2019 and indeed seemed to be a kind of anticipation of the conclusions that Pope Francis was preparing to draw from it. This led to a hue and cry, after which the pope emeritus wrote to me that he consented to my request to publish his writings, but set a mandatory condition: "For my part, I want to publish nothing more during my lifetime. The fury of the circles in Germany that are opposed to me is so strong that if anything I say appears in print, it immediately provokes a horrible uproar on their part. I want to spare myself this and to spare Christianity, too."[3]

In the same letter, Benedict apologized for not yet having started the task of revising his texts; he promised me, however, that soon he would do so. In fact, in the following months, he went to work at it. Going beyond what I had requested, he did not limit himself to reading the articles that had already been published. He significantly improved some texts, among which it is worth mentioning in particular the one on the priesthood. In a meeting that took place on June 28, 2021, the day before the seventieth

---

[2] Robert Sarah with Benedict XVI, *From the Depths of Our Hearts*, ed. Nicolas Diat, trans. Michael J. Miller (San Francisco: Ignatius Press, 2020).

[3] Letter to Elio Guerriero, dated January 13, 2021.

anniversary of his priestly ordination, he spoke to me enthusiastically about his life as a priest and emphasized the importance of the text on the priesthood that is reprinted later on here. He was satisfied with the result that he had achieved, based precisely on his personal experience. He maintained, among other things, that he had made a contribution toward overcoming a gap that had been left in the Second Vatican Council's Decree on the Ministry and Life of Priests. The ongoing work concerning the text was not yet finished. Since he wanted to give an internal structure and a sense of completeness to the anthology, he wrote several important additional essays, such as the ones on world religions and on the presence of Jesus in the Eucharist.

In short, the present volume is not just a collection of previously published texts with a few new ones added, but rather a kind of spiritual testament written in a spirit of wisdom by a fatherly heart that was always attentive to the expectations and hopes of the faithful and of all mankind. It is well known that Pope Benedict wrote in German. The translation of the texts [into Italian] was made by Pierluca Azzaro and myself. Moreover, Pope Benedict decided that the reference edition of the present book should be the Italian one.

My remaining duty is to express once again my gratitude to Pope Benedict for the confidence that he placed in me many years ago.

PREFACE

When on February 11, 2013, I announced my resignation from the ministry of the successor of Peter, I had no plan for what I would do in my new situation. I was too exhausted to be able to plan other projects. Besides, the publication of *Jesus of Nazareth: The Infancy Narratives*[1] seemed to be a logical conclusion for my theological writings.

After the election of Pope Francis, I slowly resumed my theological work. Thus, over the course of the years, a series of short and medium-length contributions took shape, and these are presented in this volume.

In the first place, there is the lecture given by me on the occasion of the dedication of the *Aula Magna* [great hall] of the Pontifical Urbaniana University on October 21, 2014. This is reprinted here unchanged.

Then I add a text to clarify the concept of the world religions with which the Christian faith wishes to enter into dialogue.

Chapter 2 addresses the topic of the nature and the development of monotheism. A short text follows on the method of the Christian-Islamic dialogue, and then a

[1] The first part in biographical order and the last in the order of publication of the trilogy dedicated to Jesus. The work was initially published in Italian in three volumes by Rizzoli; in the English edition, they had the following titles: *Jesus of Nazareth: From the Baptism in the Jordan to the Transfiguration*, translated from German by Adrian J. Walker (New York: Doubleday, 2007); *Jesus of Nazareth, Part Two: Holy Week, From the Entrance into Jerusalem to the Resurrection*, translated by Philip J. Whitmore (San Francisco: Ignatius Press, 2011); *Jesus of Nazareth: The Infancy Narratives*, translated by Philip J. Whitmore (New York: Image, 2012).

speech expressing my gratitude to the Pontifical University in Kraków for conferring on me an honorary doctorate degree. In addition to these two short texts, there is the preface that I wrote for the Russian-language edition of my *Collected Writings*, volume 11, *Theology of the Liturgy*.

In chapter 3 I reprint the text that I wrote about Jewish-Christian relations and also the exchange of letters with Rabbi Arie Folger that I conducted in August and September of 2018. Indeed, I decisively rejected the accusations concerning alleged anti-Semitic positions present in my thought. My efforts were judged in an altogether positive way by Jewish readers. I hope, therefore, that they can still make a contribution toward a good dialogue.

Chapter 4 begins with an interview that I had given at the invitation of Father Daniele Libanori. It deals with the thesis that Jesus Christ had to die in order to restore the order of being that had been overthrown by sin. The classic answer that was elaborated by Anselm of Canterbury is almost incomprehensible for us today. In the interview, I tried to show how we can understand reasonably today the motive for the suffering and death of Jesus Christ.

Next come two texts that deal with the theme of the priesthood and the Eucharist. The article on the priesthood was published in an initial form in the volume by Cardinal Sarah, *From the Depths of Our Hearts*. Later on, I reworked it and gave it a new center of gravity. The Second Vatican Council's document on the ministerial priesthood sought to show its beauty in a new way. In this context, however, one essential omission remained, caused by the situation of modern biblical exegesis. The priesthood, indeed, appears essentially as a pastoral ministry, while the *proprium sacerdotale* [essential priestly feature] was supposedly not present in New Testament pastoral ministry. I, however, was able to demonstrate that, despite this, the New Testament presbyter is a *sacerdos*, albeit in a new sense defined by the high priest Jesus Christ on the Cross. Moreover, I addressed the debate on intercommunion that from time to time is forcefully proposed again in Germany. From this resulted a more in-depth look at the presence of the Body and the Blood of Christ, and with this also a new definition of what can or cannot be meant by the expression "to eat and drink the Body and Blood of Christ".

Chapter 5 deals with moral questions. Presented here is a fundamental essay on the question of the Church and the sexual abuse scandal.

Chapter 6 contains contributions occasioned by historical anniversaries: my text on fifty years of the International Theological Commission; a remembrance of Pope Saint John Paul II on the occasion of the centennial of his birth; a complimentary address given for the seventy-fifth anniversary of the death of Father Alfred Delp. The chapter concludes with an interview on Saint Joseph, who was given to me by my parents as a patron saint for life. The older I get, the clearer the figure of my patron becomes to me. Not one word of his has been handed down to us, but rather his ability to listen and to act. I understand more and more that his silence is precisely what speaks to us and, beyond scientific knowledge, wishes to guide me to wisdom.

This volume, which collects the writings that I composed in Mater Ecclesiae Monastery, should be published after my death. I entrusted the task of editing them to Dr. Elio Guerriero, who wrote a biography of me in Italian and whom I recognize for his theological competence. Therefore I willingly entrust to him this, my final book.

Benedict XVI
Mater Ecclesiae Monastery
May 1, 2022, Feast of Saint Joseph the Worker

Chapter One

WORLD RELIGIONS
AND THE CHRISTIAN FAITH

LOVE AT THE ORIGIN OF
MISSIONARY WORK

In the first place, I would like to express my most cordial thanks to the Magnificent Rector and to the academic faculty of the Pontifical Urbaniana University, to the major officials, and to the representatives of the students for their proposal to name the renovated *Aula Magna* [great hall] after me. In particular, I would like to thank the Grand Chancellor of the university, Fernando Cardinal Filoni, for having welcomed this initiative. It is a cause of great joy for me to be able to be ever present in this way to the work of the Pontifical Urbaniana University.

Over the course of several visits that I was able to make as prefect of the Congregation for the Doctrine of the Faith, I always remained struck by the atmosphere of universality that one breathes at this university, in which young people coming from practically all the countries in the world prepare themselves for service to the Gospel in the contemporary world. Today, too, I see in my mind's eye before me, in the renovated hall, a community made up of many young men and women who make us perceive vividly the stupendous reality of the Catholic Church.

"Catholic": this attribute of the Church, which has been part of the profession of faith from the most ancient

The message "Love at the Origin of Missionary Work" was read on the occasion of the dedication of the renovated *Aula Magna* [great hall] of the Pontifical Urbaniana University, which was named after Benedict XVI on October 21, 2014.

times, bears within it something of Pentecost. It reminds us that the Church of Jesus Christ has never been concerned with only one nation or only one culture, but that from the start it was destined for humanity. The last words that Jesus spoke to his disciples were "Make disciples of all nations" (Mt 28:19). And at the moment of Pentecost, the apostles spoke in all languages and, thus, were able to manifest, by the power of the Holy Spirit, the complete fullness of their faith.

From then on, the Church really has grown on all the continents. Your presence, dear students, reflects the universal face of the Church. The prophet Zechariah had announced a messianic kingdom that would extend from sea to sea and would be a kingdom of peace (Zech 9:9–10). And indeed, wherever the Eucharist is celebrated and people, at the Lord's initiative, become among themselves one Body, something of the peace that Jesus Christ promised to give to his disciples is present. You, dear friends, are coworkers of this peace, and in a divided and violent world, it becomes more and more urgent to build up and to preserve this peace. This is why the work of your university is so important, in which you aim to learn to know Jesus Christ more closely so as to be able to become his witnesses.

The Risen Lord commissioned his apostles, and through them the disciples of all times, to bring his message to the ends of the earth and to make disciples of all men. The Second Vatican Council, repeating in its decree *Ad gentes* a tradition present in all centuries, highlighted the profound reasons for this missionary task and thus assigned it with renewed force to the Church of today.

"But is this really still valid?" many people wonder, both within and outside the Church. Is it true that missionary work is still of current interest? Would it not be more appropriate to meet one another in the dialogue among the world religions and to serve together the cause of peace in the world? The counterquestion is: Can dialogue replace missionary work? Many today, indeed, have the notion that the world religions should respect one another and, in the dialogue between them, become a common force for peace. In this way of thinking, most often the presupposition is that the different religions are variants of one and the same reality; that "religion" is the common genus that takes on different forms depending on the different cultures, but expresses the same reality anyway. The question of truth, the one that originally motivated Christians more than anything else, is bracketed off here. It is presupposed that the authentic truth about God, in the final analysis, is unattainable and that at most we can make present the ineffable only with a variety of symbols. This renunciation of the truth seems realistic and useful for peace among the religions in the world. Nevertheless, it is lethal for the faith. Indeed, the faith loses its binding character and its seriousness if everything is reduced to symbols that are basically interchangeable, capable of referring only from a distance to the inaccessible mystery of the divine.

Dear friends, you see that the question of missionary work confronts us not only with the fundamental questions of the faith but also with the question of what man is. Within the limits of these short words of greeting, obviously I cannot try to analyze exhaustively this set of problems that profoundly concerns all of us today. I would like, therefore, at least to indicate the direction in which our thought should proceed. I will do this by setting out from two different points of departure.

I

1. The common opinion is that world religions are, so to speak, simply side by side, like the continents and the

individual countries on the map. But this is not accurate. The world religions are in movement at the historical level, just as nations and cultures are in movement. There are expectant religions. Tribal religions are of this sort: they have their historical moment and yet are expectantly awaiting a greater encounter that will bring them to their fullness. We, as Christians, are convinced that, in silence, they are awaiting the encounter with Jesus Christ, the light that comes from him, which alone can lead them completely to their truth. And Christ awaits them. The encounter with him is not the intrusion of something foreign that destroys their own culture and their own history. It is, rather, an entrance into something greater toward which they are traveling. Therefore this encounter is always simultaneously a purification and a maturation. Moreover, the encounter is always reciprocal. Christ awaits their history, their wisdom, their vision of things. Today we see with increasing clarity another aspect, too: whereas Christianity has in many respects grown weary in the countries where its great history has unfolded, and some branches of the large tree that grew from the mustard seed of the Gospel have become dry and fallen to the ground, new life springs from the encounter of the expectant religions with Christ. Where there was only weariness before, new dimensions of the faith are manifested and bring joy.

2. Religion in itself is not a monolithic phenomenon. Several dimensions must always be distinguished in it. On the one hand, there is the greatness of stretching out beyond the world toward the eternal God. But on the other hand, this greatness contains elements that sprang from the history of mankind and from its practice of religion. Among them, of course, we may find beautiful and noble things, but also base and destructive things, where man's selfishness has taken possession of religion and turned it

into a self-enclosure instead of an opening. Therefore religion is never simply a purely positive or purely negative phenomenon: in it both aspects are mixed. In its beginnings, the Christian mission perceived very forcefully, above all, the negative elements of the pagan religions that it confronted. For this reason, the Christian proclamation was at first extremely critical of religion. Only by overcoming their traditions, which in part it considered even demonic, could the faith display its renovating force. On the basis of elements of this sort, the Calvinist theologian Karl Barth contrasted religion and faith, judging the first in an absolutely negative way as the arbitrary behavior of man who tries by himself to grasp God. Dietrich Bonhoeffer adopted this attitude, declaring that he was in favor of a Christianity "without religion". No doubt this is a unilateral view that cannot be accepted. And yet it is correct to affirm that every religion, in order to remain just, always has to be critical of religion at the same time. Clearly this has been true of the Christian faith from its very beginning, in accord with its nature. On the one hand, it looks with great respect at the interior expectation and the interior wealth of the world religions, but on the other hand, it sees in a critical way what is negative. It goes without saying that again and again the Christian faith must display that critical faculty with respect to its own religious history, too. For us Christians, Jesus Christ is the *Logos* of God, the light that helps us to distinguish between the nature of religion and its distortion.

3. In our time, the voices of those who want to convince us that religion as such is outmoded are becoming louder and louder. Only critical reason, they say, should direct human action. Behind concepts like this is the conviction that with positivistic thought, reason in all its purity has definitively taken control. In reality, even this

way of thinking and living is historically conditioned and connected with specific historical cultures. To consider this way of thinking as the only valid one ultimately belittles man by taking away essential dimensions of his existence. Man becomes smaller, not greater, when there is no longer room for an *ethos* that, in accord with his authentic nature, moves beyond pragmatism, when there is no longer room for a gaze that is turned toward God. The proper place for positivistic reason is in the great technological and economic fields of activity, and yet it does not exhaust all that is human. So it is up to us who believe to open wide again and again the doors that lead beyond mere technology and pure pragmatism to the whole greatness of our existence, to the encounter with the living God.

II

1. These reflections, though a bit difficult, ought to show that even today, in a profoundly changed world, the task of communicating the Gospel of Jesus Christ to others remains reasonable. And nevertheless there is also a second, simpler way to justify this task today. Joy needs to be communicated. Love needs to be communicated. Truth needs to be communicated. Someone who has received a great joy cannot simply keep it for himself; he has to hand it on. The same is true for the gift of love and for the gift of recognizing the truth that is manifested. When Andrew met Christ, he could not help telling his brother: "We have found the Messiah" (Jn 1:41). And when the same encounter had been granted to Philip, he could not help telling Nathanael that he had found the one about whom Moses and the prophets had written (Jn 1:45). Let us proclaim Jesus Christ, not in order to gain as many

members as possible for our community, much less for the sake of power. Let us speak about him because we feel that we must hand on this joy that was given to us. We will be credible announcers of Jesus Christ when we have truly encountered him in the depths of our being, when, through the encounter with him, we have received the gift of the great experience of truth, love, and joy.

2. Part of the nature of religion is the profound tension between the mystical offering to God, in which we give ourselves totally to him, and responsibility for our neighbor and for the world created by God. Martha and Mary are always inseparable, even though, from time to time, the emphasis may fall on one or the other. The meeting point between the two poles is the love in which we touch God and his creatures at the same time. "We know and believe the love God has for us" (1 Jn 4:16): this sentence expresses the authentic nature of Christianity. Love, which is realized and reflected in manifold ways in the saints of all times, is the authentic proof of the truth of Christianity.

WHAT IS RELIGION?

An Attempt to Define the Concept of Religion

When we try to clarify the essence of religion, the first point that emerges is that religion exists only in actual religions. There is no abstract nature of religion, but rather only concrete forms of religion. This seems to leave the attempt to find methods of dialogue in a blind alley. World religions, indeed, appear like a building that embraces continents of space and time. Upon closer inspection, though, it is evident that religions, beyond the continents, appear as grandiose constructions that moreover, cannot be presented in a static way, but historically are found to be in movement, whereby they ultimately tend to surpass themselves. In this movement, nevertheless, they are not destroyed, but rather purified and brought back to their more authentic nature.

The so-called tribal religions (which once were simply described as paganism) recognize gods that are ordered to particular areas of life. The fertility cults are the most visible ones. Their members joyfully venerate the mystery of fertility and thus receive it at the same time in a way that is ever new. Therefore the essential contents of these cults are diligence in preserving fertility, gratitude for the preservation thereof, and rejoicing over it. In so doing, however, the followers automatically and everywhere

"What Is Religion?", previously unpublished, was completed on March 19, 2022.

reach a point of ecstatic abuse, in which the divine and the human elements are intertwined with each other and thus lose their proper dignity. In this way, these cults have led to the destruction of entire societies, thus calling into question the very nature of religion. The struggle against these cults with their temptations broadly defines the relation of the biblical faith with regard to religions.

Naturally there is also a positive side to these religions, inasmuch as they are ordered to the preservation and the fertility of the earth. In the society of late antiquity, they appear as nothing less than the essence of paganism, which now is manifested in an altogether positive way in propitiatory processions, in rituals and similar gestures. Christianity, which at the start was unacquainted with these devotional forms and opposed to the religiosity of the countryside, finally had to adopt, purify, and correct many elements from this setting, but also to accept new overtures and concrete forms of devotion. The so-called *litaniae maiores* [major litanies] were preserved as prayers of supplication down to the threshold of the present era. What started as paganism, which was opposed to the faith, is today a kind of Christian vision of life and of the world, which unfortunately is destined to die. What was apparently pagan, which at the start seemingly had to be eliminated, ultimately contributed to the representation of a life that is received ever anew as coming from God.

I would like to recall here another particularly important area: it concerns the way of dealing with sickness and death. In pagan ritual, there are profoundly moving words and gestures, but also arbitrariness that exploits the challenge posed by sickness and death so as to exert its power in turn. Today as in the past, the power of magicians defiles the face of the tribal religions. One essential expression of the relation with the dead in all tribal religions is ancestor worship, which for the most part was considered in the past to be in opposition to the Christian vision of life and death. Based on his experience, Horst Bürkle proposed a new appropriation and presentation of ancestor worship that to me seems worth considering. He shows that the individualism that developed in the West and puts up the strongest resistance with regard to ancestor worship is, in reality, opposed also to the Christian anthropology that sees us as being protected within the Mystical Body of Christ. Man's bond with Christ is not only an I-Thou relation but creates a new We. Communion with Jesus Christ introduces us into the Body of Christ, in other words, into the great community of all those who belong to the Lord, and therefore it extends beyond the boundary between death and life. In this sense, communion with those who have preceded us is an essential part of being a Christian. It enables us to find forms of communion with the dead, which perhaps in Africa manifest themselves differently from the way they do in Europe, but in any case allow us to bring about a richly meaningful transformation of ancestor worship.

But now the question arises of how faith in one God can overcome the world of the gods. The Divine Word missionary Wilhelm Schmidt, throughout his life's work, maintained the thesis that faith in the one God arose at the origin of the history of religion and gradually became increasingly obscured by the multiple deities, until it was able to suppress the gods once again. In the end, he himself admitted that such a development cannot be proved. Rather, somehow it was always known that the gods are not simply the plural of God. God is a God in the singular. He exists solely in unity. The plurality of the gods works at another level. In fact, the world with its different areas is ruled by deities that can dominate only their one part.

As for the one God, what Erik Peterson wrote about him in his important early monograph *Monotheism as a Political Problem* is true: "Le roi règne, mais il ne gouverne pas" [The king reigns, but he does not govern]. Over the course of the history of religions, God was considered as a monarch who does have power over everything but does not exercise it. The one true God needs no worship, because he does not threaten anyone and does not need the help of anyone. The goodness and the power of the one true God determine at the same time his insignificance. He does not need us, and man thinks that he does not need God. With the proliferation of faith in the gods there was increasingly a yearning that the true God with his power could liberate man from the regime of fear within which faith in the gods had developed extensively. According to the conviction of Christians, this was precisely what happened with Jesus: the one God entered into the history of religions and deposed the gods. Henri de Lubac especially has demonstrated that Christianity was perceived as liberation from the fear in which the power of the gods had shackled man. Basically the mighty world of the gods crumbled because the one God entered the scene and set a limit to their power.

I tried to describe this event in a little more detail in the collection of writings *Gott in Welt* [God in the world] published on the occasion of the sixtieth birthday of Karl Rahner, and I was able to establish that there are two ways out of faith in the gods. First, the monotheistic religions rooted in Abraham, in which the one God as a person causes the whole world. Besides this, there is a second way out, namely, the mystical religions with Hinayana Buddhism as a central form. Here there is no one personal God, but rather even the one God is dissolved and becomes evanescent. The way of Buddha tends toward annihilation. In reality, this severe form of mystical dissolution of all individual figures did not prevail, but in recent times it always remained as a final description and acquired a strong attractive force precisely in the once-Christian cultures of Europe. In the German-speaking world, it found an expression in the sentence attributed to Karl Rahner: "The Christian of tomorrow will be a mystic, or else he will no longer exist."

Apparently this envisages an interiorization and an inner deepening of the faith. I will not attempt to clarify what Rahner meant to say by this sentence. For many, on the contrary, it conceals only the program to present all concrete forms of faith as secondary in order to arrive ultimately at an impersonal piety, like the one that Luise Rinser [1911–2002, author of novels and short stories] mentions as the superior form of being Christian that she has followed in the meantime.

The German writer explained to me personally that the purpose of publishing her correspondence with Karl Rahner was to demonstrate that she was a mystic and that the long spiritual journey that she made with Rahner during the conciliar and postconciliar years flowed ultimately into the mystical explanation of Christianity. It did not become clear to me to what extent Luise Rinser meant to involve Rahner in the transformation of Christianity into a mystical religion. In any case, she meant to offer an explanation of Rahner's famous phrase as an opening toward the future.

As a matter of fact, such an interpretation of Christianity contradicts its innermost intention and its concrete historical configuration. For a Christian, the God who in Jesus Christ binds himself heart and hand to us men and who endured being human for us and among us even unto death and beyond death, is the center of Christianity. The whole quarrel in the history of religions between God and the gods does not end with the fact that God himself finally vanishes like a fetish. Rather, it ends with the victory of the one true God over the gods who are not God. It ends consequently with the gift of love that presupposes the personal being of God. Therefore, for man, too, it ends with the fact that he fully becomes a person by accepting the gift of being loved by God and by handing it on.

Chapter Two

FUNDAMENTAL ELEMENTS OF THE CHRISTIAN RELIGION

MONOTHEISM AND TOLERANCE

After addressing the relation between monotheism and
intolerance for the first time in an essentially superficial
way, Eckhard Nordhofen dealt with the question at length
in his extensive monograph *Corpora. Die anarchische Kraft
des Monotheismus.*[1] Nevertheless, I had the impression that
the purely historical aspect can be studied in greater depth.
That was the origin of this essay, in which I seek to give a
glimpse of the complexity of what happened. I think that
the points where the distant past reflects on the present,
too, emerge automatically and hence do not have to be
discussed analytically. This is true especially about the last
paragraph, in which, viewed superficially, the great power
of Hellenist culture and religion—understood as a modern force of tolerance—runs across the marginal and irre-
ducibly intolerant phenomenon of a group that is hostile
to an enlightened view, i.e., Judaism, and for that reason
becomes in its turn intolerant. From today's perspective,
however, another evaluation of the situation at that time is
possible: we Christians, who decisively regard the essential
form of our faith as something that sprang from Judaism,
find ourselves victims precisely of a growing intolerance
that is practiced in the very name of tolerance. In this essay
of mine, I have deliberately refrained from speaking about

"Monotheism and Tolerance" was completed on December 29, 2018.

[1] [Bodies: the anarchic power of monotheism], (Freiburg im Breisgau:
Herder, 2018).

the current relevance of the past; I leave this task to the reader's reflection.

The complexity of the process, however, begins very quickly. The famous episode of the golden calf (Ex 32), for example, is not simply about the profession of God's oneness, but about Israel's relation of fidelity to its God, which failed because the people had reduced God to a statue. The purpose of this passage is not to defend the oneness of God but, rather, to condemn the infidelity of Israel, which through the covenant had entered into a particular type of relation of fidelity with this God.

An examination of the understanding of "monotheism" in the Books of Joshua, Judges, and Kings, respectively, would lead us too far afield. Therefore I would like to analyze briefly only the text of Joshua 24:15–28, because there we find a presentation of Israel's relation with its God that is decisive for all that follows. Israel freely accepts the exclusive covenant with God when the opportunity is given explicitly to it to reject it and thus to be released from the obligations toward him that are inherent in the covenant. This exclusive bond with Yahweh, and the resulting exclusion of all the other gods, as well as the struggle against them, is not presented as a consequence of an abstract monotheism, but rather results solely from the concrete covenant relationship with the God who for Israel is the one God and who effectively can claim exclusively for himself a land that seemed to belong to other gods. It must be added, on the other hand, that, at another stage of sacred history, intolerance toward the peoples who previously had inhabited the Promised Land appears with a different motivation. There it says that those peoples had defiled the territories so much with the abominations desired by their deities—particularly with human sacrifices—that they no longer had any right to that land;

and it says that Yahweh had given that land to Israel so that its people could live there according to his Law, thus restoring the land to its dignity. In fact, considerable parts of the preceding population had remained on that land, and as a result Israel did not live fully according to God's will, teaching the other peoples also to live uprightly. Instead, the opposite happened: Israel strayed from the way of life that had been given to it and conformed to the life-style of those peoples. In this case, too, on the other hand, what defines their "intolerance" toward the other peoples is not quite an abstract monotheism, but rather a bond between morality and faith, which silently calls reason as well to testify to the justice of God's action.

Essential perspectives concerning the question of the relation between monotheism and tolerance can be found also in the story of Solomon and the women for love of whom he had shrines built in honor of their deities. Solomon appears, on the one hand, as the ideal sovereign, as the master of wisdom who by means of the wisdom books continues to speak to his people and more generally to humanity. But, on the other hand, success had seduced him, leading him to an unbridled life-style—part of which was a large harem—which also included building shrines of the pagan world. Following modern criteria, one might say that Solomon was an enlightened monarch who granted space to the various religions, thus allowing for their reciprocal tolerance. The official historiography of Israel takes a conflicting position with regard to him. In one respect, Solomon is presented as the great and wise king to whom a forty-year reign was granted. But at the same time, right during his reign, the subsequent division between Israel and Judah begins, and his religious toler-ance is deplored as an abandonment of wisdom and as a fall into the utter folly of idolatrous worship. The story of Saint Stephen, in the New Testament, shows how the ostentatious temple, which Solomon erected in place of the sacred tent, spiritually symbolizes a transition to a false piety, because the true God does not dwell in buildings of stone but remains the itinerant God.

Matters stand quite differently during the reign of Ahab. For love of his pagan wife, Jezebel, he grants to her divinities all the space she wants; for this very reason, he appears as the prototype of the bad sovereign, even though from the events narrated it is clear that, within the limits of what was then possible to do and could be expected, he was a good sovereign for his people: when he was mortally wounded in the war against Syria, all Israel mourned his death. The dramatic clash between monotheism (faith in the one God) and the falsehood of idolatry took place in the conflict between Elijah and Jezebel. As a result of Jezebel's policy, Elijah remained the only prophet of the one God, the God of Sinai, and was opposed by the 450 prophets of Baal. God's judgment, which was acknowledged by both parties, was executed by Elijah with the slaughter of all the prophets of Baal. The victory thus won in fact by monotheism seemed to put Elijah on the side of right, but the actual balance of power threatened Elijah, soul and body, and compelled him to flee. He traveled back on the road toward the mountain of God, Sinai, to receive new instructions there. According to an interpretation that remains controversial, the encounter with God that was granted to him should be understood as a condemnation of the violence employed in the struggle against the deities. God is not in the fire and not in the storm; his presence is perceived in the whispering of a light breeze.

Around three hundred years later, at the beginning of the activity of Deutero-Isaiah, we encounter again the mysterious voice that announces the end of the Exile, the liberation of Israel. A half millennium later we hear it once more, and now it has become the voice of a man, John the Baptist, in whom is fulfilled also the passage from the Old to the New Testament. As the meaning of the voice becomes progressively concrete, it becomes clear what the revelation to Elijah on Sinai means in the final analysis: God conquers, not in the violence that Elijah had practiced, but in the suffering Servant of God in whom God himself intervenes in history. Even though it remains an open question, what original meaning should be assigned to the theophany granted to Elijah, its re-presentation in Isaiah and in John the Baptist allows us, however, to affirm that it announces a new and mysterious way of framing the question about God's power and powerlessness in the world.

Even though Elisha did not continue that policy of violence, he himself does not seem to have understood this answer. Instead, the policy of violence was continued in the reign of Jehu, with an extremely bloody regime that led to the massacre of the entire house of Ahab. Jehu stated, on the other hand, that in this way he was following Elisha's direction. Sacred Scripture does not say whether Elisha knew about that violent regime and, if so, whether he expressed an opinion about it. In any case, it is clear that the bloody rule of Jehu, notwithstanding the fact that Elisha called him to that task, had nothing more to do with monotheism—the alternative between God and the many Baals—but rather exclusively concerned a power struggle in Israel.

Let us attempt, however, a better analysis of the individual passages of the narration. The terrifying massacre by Elijah should be understood as an answer to the question about the living God. The slaughter is perpetrated by Elijah in the silence of the Baals and in the mighty response of his God. Therefore, it should not be interpreted as a victory of monotheism over polytheism. In the given situation, it instead takes the form of the concrete response to the threat menacing the faith that Israel received from its ancestors. The faith of the fathers is defended against the arrogance of Queen Jezebel, who would like to allow room only for her gods. Jezebel, the other protagonist of the drama of Carmel, has brought her gods with her and sees them as the embodiment of her power. She is rebuked above all for treating Israel's faith, represented by Naboth, with the cynicism of power. Naboth sees the vineyard that he inherited from his ancestors as the gift of the earth that the God of Israel promised to his people and that for him is represented concretely by that vineyard. The vineyard is for him his participation in the promise, the gift of the land received from his ancestors and inherited by him. Ahab's generous offer to give him in exchange a vineyard of equal or greater value does not matter to him: what matters for him is the heritage of his fathers. Jezebel opposes this faith with the arrogance of power, which considers even defamation as an obvious means to an end. The Old Testament author sees in this the essence of the religion of Baal and sees expressed here the fundamental contrast with faith in the God of the fathers. The cults of Baal are fertility cults, in which the boundary between God and man dissolves: the divine is dragged down, and its dignity is distorted in an incomparable dissipation. In this sense, the cults of Baal prove to be the genuine reason for the moral destruction of the peoples, from which the land must be liberated.

On this basis, it is then possible to understand the meaning of the first commandment of the Decalogue, which is considered quite clearly the authentic, essential fundamental requirement of the divine law, which the following commandments merely explain in concrete terms: the one God is above all human realities. In the pure transcendence that is his own, he is at the same time the guarantor of human dignity. The struggle in favor of the living God against Baal is a struggle for human justice, which is expressed concretely by the fourth to the tenth commandments. Here the question about tolerance or intolerance of religions still remains open. In this sense, it seems to me that no decisive conclusion can be drawn from Elijah's action on Mount Carmel with regard to the question of the tolerance or intolerance of monotheism. The journey to Mount Sinai, indeed, already unlocks a new concept, which, however, will be developed and affirmed only later on.

Let us try now to determine more precisely the relation between Israel's faith in God and the religion of Baal. The characteristic that is decisive for Israel's faith is the fact that only one God stands in front of the people of Israel and all the other peoples on earth. His relation to the world as a whole can be described as transcendence. For the fertility religions with their Baals, on the contrary, the important thing is that there is no insurmountable boundary between the world of the divine and the world of man. Thus, the essence of religion does not consist in the obedience of man to the transcendent God (as it does for Israel), but rather precisely in the intermingling of human things with those that are divine. At the core of religion is the great mystery of fertility, which in [primitive] religions is relished and experienced in its magnificence as well as in its destructive force. Since by virtue of the God of Israel the rites that intermingle the divine and the human are considered to be arrogance and, in the final analysis, the destruction of the world and of mankind, Israel must reject all that. Somewhat schematically, we can therefore say that the fertility cults are an identity religion, while we can describe the adoration of the transcendent God as a religion of obedience. The content of this obedience consists, as we saw, in the Decalogue—which in a certain sense can be considered the authentic representation of God. By putting it into practice, man becomes the image of God and like him.

A look at the Book of Amos provides a further clarification. The important thing, it seems to me, is above all the way in which Amos presents himself to the king. Amaziah, the priest of Bethel, the central sanctuary of the northern kingdom, says to Amos: "Go, flee away to the land of Judah...; but never again prophesy at Bethel, for it is the king's sanctuary, and it is a temple of the kingdom" (Amos 7:12–13). Equally important is Amos' reply: "I am no prophet, nor a prophet's son; but I am a herdsman, and a dresser of sycamore trees" (Amos 7:14). This signifies the independence of God's message from politics and signifies the prophet's freedom with regard to political power. In this specific case it signifies even more. Indeed, one peculiarity of the concrete situation of Israel at that time is the opposition between rural population and urban economic development, with the growing wealth of the cities and the power of their social structures, which almost inevitably leads the population of the countryside to impoverishment. So, in this specific case, Amos became a champion of social equality and of justice. Just as God's message does not depend on any human authority, so too it signifies a commitment to justice with regard to all. When we analyze the Pentateuch and the historical books of Israel, a third element then emerges: solicitude for the widows, for the orphans, and for the strangers. They are particularly loved and protected by God.

Furthermore, yet another aspect should be considered. The Book of Amos begins with a series of threats of chastisement against the nations: calamities are dramatically foretold to them for the misdeeds that they have perpetrated. Threats of chastisements against other nations are common outside of Israel, too. The prophet turns the usual scheme completely upside down here with the novelty that God's judgment culminates in the judgment against his own people.[2] In the final analysis, the purpose of God's action is the salvation of all nations: the universality that is foretold here can be considered a fundamental motive of God's action in the Old Testament.

It is clear, in any case, that it is not accurate to consider monotheism a label that can be applied to different historical situations and that can be associated with contemporary concepts such as tolerance or intolerance.

Let us take a look finally at the time of the Exile and at the Maccabees. Only during the time of the Exile did monotheism develop completely in Israel. Until then it was certainly clear that Israel had one God and that all the other gods were idols. But whether they existed and how they were to be classified ontologically were questions that remained outside the scope of Israel's interests. Now, though, Israel had been robbed of its land, and this normally put an end to the divinity of a country or of a nation. A god who was not capable of defending his people and his land could not be a god. In Israel, on the contrary, the opposite train of thought was followed. The God of Abraham, Isaac, and Jacob, the God of Sinai, ruled all the earth. He could send his people to Egypt for centuries, could snatch them from the power of Pharaoh, and could lead them through the desert to the Promised Land; and even there he could cause them to be defeated and exiled to Babylon. He was neither the God of a specific land nor merely the God of that specific people. During the time of the Exile, the concept of creation becomes central. God is

[2] Erich Zenger, *Einleitung ins Alte Testament* (Stuttgart: Kohlhammer, 1996).

the Creator of heaven and of earth. He alone created the world from nothing. He alone is truly God.

Israel's faith confronts us with this paradox: the one and only God above all the gods chose Israel for himself, drawing it to himself with his love, without being bound to it in any way. He needs no sanctuary because all the earth belongs to him. It is magnificent, as the psalmist says, that all the earth is only a little thing that he holds in his hands. God can use the mighty of the earth for his purposes and choose as his servant Cyrus, who sends Israel back to its land. It is clear that in this situation Israel could not think of claiming this God for itself with political intolerance. In the situation of the Exile, Israel can only place itself confidently in God's hands. He alone has power over all reality.

This also means, however, that in its dispute with the nations, now Israel appeals also to common reason: it speaks about the God who is comprehensible not only in the faith of Israel. Obviously the polytheistic cults do not think of themselves as having a rational foundation, while the one God in whom Israel believes and whom it adores wishes to be ascertained and understood in a rational view of the world, too. The ridicule of the gods that have ears and do not hear, that have eyes and do not see, may be considered rude in a certain respect; and yet it expresses precisely this new step that has been taken toward full monotheism. This prepared for the encounter with Greek thought, for which the Septuagint offered itself as an instrument, and which is then explicitly taken up again in the late wisdom literature. It was a preparation also for the encounter (made definitively in Christianity) between philosophical thought and the faith of Israel.

The thought of Socrates, who was pious and critical at the same time, had in its own way the effect of unveiling the illusory character of the gods. Today we face the opposite movement of the human mind. Modern thought no longer wants to acknowledge the truth of being, but wants to acquire power over being. It wants to reshape the world according to its own needs and desires. With this orientation—not to the truth but to power—we no doubt touch on the true problem of the present time, to which we will have to return at the conclusion.

Let us take another look at the Maccabees. From the victories of Alexander the Great had sprung a large Hellenic space that during the reigns of the Diadochi kings took on a cultural and political form. Traditional ways of life that stood in the way of the unity that was being established had to be abolished in favor of that monolithic culture that held everything together. It was clear, therefore, that among others, the Jewish ways of life prescribed by the Pentateuch (circumcision, dietary precepts, etc.) had to disappear, too, because they were not compatible with the modern monolithic state; just as Israel's faith, lifestyle, and language were not compatible with the new uniform cultural model.

A non-negligible sector of the Israelites obviously welcomed with joy their fusion with the modern life-style enlightened by Hellenism; others shunned it, for lack of alternatives. But both the faith of Israel and its ways of life, which included also its language, inevitably had to react sooner or later. The First Book of the Maccabees describes effectively how Mattathias, an authoritative and highly esteemed man, rebelled against those claims, rejected the promises of the new society, and opposed the king's ambassador. He resisted the grand promises of wealth that were made to him, as well as the request to offer sacrifices to the idols, saying: "Even if all the nations that live under the rule of the king obey him, ... departing each one from the religion of his fathers..., yet I and

my sons and my brothers will live by the covenant of our
fathers.... We will not obey the king's words by turning
aside from our religion to the right hand or to the left"
(1 Mac 2:19–22).

After these words were spoken, when a Jew was about
to sacrifice on the pagan altar according to the king's
request, Mattathias, seeing this, "burned with zeal.... He
ran and killed him upon the altar. At the same time he
killed the king's officer" (1 Mac 2:24–25). The Book of
the Maccabees justifies this deed as a recovery of the "zeal"
about which the Book of Numbers had spoken in relating
the act of Phinehas. The "zeal" now rises to the level of a
fundamental principle in the revolt against the monolithic
Hellenistic civilization: Mattathias fled to the mountains,
and many followed him. Once it had arisen in this way,
the Maccabean movement was able to oppose the military
power of the state and to establish a new state of Israel
founded on faith, in which the Temple of Jerusalem was
reestablished, also.

The Maccabean movement is founded on Israel's decisive
fidelity to its own identity. This fidelity is not understood
at all as a rigid attachment to ancient but now outmoded
traditions. Since the God of Israel is the true God who
can be known rationally also, fidelity to his laws is fidelity
to the truth. Certainly the spirit of this movement is not
captured by slapping the label of monotheistic intolerance
on it. Rather, this is a confrontation between the intolerance of the modern state (together with the only lifestyle
that it considers valid) and fidelity to the faith of the fathers
(together with the way of life that is proper to it).

A look at the contemporary scene is called for here. The
modern state in the Western world, in fact, on the one
hand, considers itself a great force of tolerance that breaks
with the foolish, prerational traditions of all religions.

Moreover, with its radical manipulation of man and distortion of the sexes through gender ideology, it opposes Christianity in a particular way. This dictatorial claim always to be right, due to an apparent rationality, requires the abandonment of Christian anthropology and of the way of life that follows from it, which is deemed prerational. The intolerance of this apparent modernity with respect to the Christian faith has not yet turned into open persecution and yet manifests itself in an increasingly authoritarian way and legislates accordingly, aiming to achieve the extinction of what is essentially Christian. The attitude of Mattathias—"We will not obey the king's words" (modern legislation)—is that of Christians. The "zeal" of Mattathias, however, is not the form in which Christian zeal is expressed. Authentic "zeal" takes its essential form from the Cross of Jesus Christ.

Finally, let us try to draw some sort of conclusion from this rapid review of several stages of the history of the Old Testament faith in the one God.

First of all, we can state without further ado that historically monotheism appears in many different modes. Therefore it cannot be defined unambiguously according to the same modern criteria as a monolithic phenomenon. One arrives at monotheism, in the strict sense of the term according to its modern usage, only when it is associated with the question of the truth. In Israel, this passage occurs fundamentally starting with the Exile, even though not in the true and proper sense of philosophical reflection. The revolutionary event, from the perspective of the history of religions, occurs with the Christian acceptance of faith in the one God, which had been prepared throughout the Mediterranean basin by the group of "God-fearing men". The definitive affirmation of the universal claim of the one God was, on the other hand, still hindered by the fact that

this one God had bound himself to Israel and that therefore he was fully accessible only in Israel; the pagans could
adore him together with Israel, but could not belong to
him completely. Only the Christian faith, with its universality that Paul had secured definitively, now allowed that
the one God could be adored concretely also in the God of
Israel who revealed himself. The encounter brought about
by the Christian mission between the "God of the philos-
ophers" and the concrete God of the Hebrew religion is
the event that revolutionizes universal history.

In the final analysis, the success of this mission is based
precisely on that encounter. Thus the Christian faith was
able to present itself in history as the *religio vera*, the true
religion. Christianity's claim to universality is based on the
opening of religion to philosophy. This is how to explain
why, in the mission that developed in Christian antiquity,
Christianity did not conceive of itself as a religion but,
rather, in the first place as a continuation of philosophical thought, in other words, of man's search for truth.
This, unfortunately, has been increasingly forgotten in the
modern era. The Christian religion is now considered a
continuation of the world religions and is itself considered
one religion among or above the others. Thus the "seeds
of the Logos", about which Clement of Alexandria speaks
as the tendency of pre-Christian history toward Christ, are
generally identified with the religions, whereas Clement
of Alexandria himself considered them part of the process of philosophical thought in which human thought
advances by trial and error toward Christ.

Let us return to the question of tolerance. The preceding discussion means that Christianity understands itself
essentially as truth and bases on this its claim to universality. But precisely at this point the contemporary critique
of Christianity intervenes, which considers the claim to

truth intolerant in itself. Truth and tolerance seem to be in contradiction. The intolerance of Christianity would then be closely connected with its claim to truth. Underlying this concept is the suspicion that the truth is dangerous in itself. For this reason, the basic tendency of modernity moves ever more clearly toward a form of culture that is independent of the truth. Postmodern culture—which makes man his own creator and disputes the original gift of creation—manifests a will to recreate the world contrary to its truth. We have already seen previously how this very attitude necessarily leads to intolerance.

But as for the relation between truth and tolerance, tolerance is anchored to the very nature of truth. While referring to the revolt of the Maccabees, we saw how a society that sets itself against the truth is totalitarian and, therefore, profoundly intolerant. As far as the truth is concerned, I would simply like to defer to Origen. "Christ wins no victory over someone who is unwilling. He conquers only by persuasion. Not for nothing is he the Word of God."[3] But at the end, as an authentic counterbalance to all forms of intolerance, stands Jesus Christ crucified. The victory of faith can always be achieved only in communion with Jesus Crucified. The theology of the Cross is the Christian response to the question about freedom and violence; and in fact, even historically, Christianity won its victories only thanks to the persecuted and never when it sided with the persecutors.

[3] *Patrologia Graeca* 12, 1133 B.

THE CHRISTIAN-ISLAMIC
DIALOGUE

Constantly I have occasion to observe that not only are the
Christian-Islamic dialogues characterized, thematically, by
an insufficient knowledge of the sacred texts of Christianity
and of Islam, but even structurally they are framed incor-
rectly. It is emphasized, on the one hand, that both the
Qur'an and the Christian Bible speak about God's mercy,
and therefore the imperative to love is present, and, on
the other hand, that violence, too, is taught by both texts.
And so, as though setting oneself above the two religions
and their sources, it is stated: there is some good and some
bad in both; it is therefore necessary for us to interpret the
texts in terms of a hermeneutic of love by then opposing
violence, with regard to both.

This approach disregards fundamental structural differences that refer to different levels.

1. The Qur'an [Koran] is one book that developed in
various situations over the course of Mohammad's life.
This book, however, is considered, not as the work of a
man, but as being directly inspired by God and therefore
makes the claim, in every part of it, to possess an authority
coming from God.

Three fundamental elements structurally differentiate
the Christian Bible from the Qur'an:

"The Christian-Islamic Dialogue" was completed on March 1, 2018, and
was previously unpublished.

—The Sacred Scripture of the Christians is not *one book* but, rather, a collection, which matured over an approximately thousand-year history, of different books with a different theological claim. According to the faith of the Jews and also of the Christians, they were not dictated directly by God but, rather, coming from him in a different way, are an interpretation of the journey that the community of the people of God makes under his guidance. They are the Word of God mediated by the word of man. Their authority is different, and the individual parts can be understood correctly only in the totality of the journey that they represent.

—Within this diversified millennial literature, there is for Christians a further qualitative subdivision, the one between Old and New Testament. The New Testament, too, is a collection of different books, which can be understood only as a whole and in terms of this whole. For Jews, only the Old Testament is "Bible". For Christians, however, it is possible to grasp the Old Testament correctly only in terms of the new interpretation that it had in the words and actions of Jesus Christ. The New Testament gives valid witness to this interpretation. The two collections of texts—the Old and the New Testaments—refer to each other in such a way that the New Testament is the interpretive key to the Old. From a Christian perspective, only in terms of the New Testament can we establish what the lasting theological significance of the Old Testament is.

—For this reason, it is not possible to speak about a verbal inspiration of the Bible. The meaning and the authority of the individual parts are correctly gathered only *from the Bible as a whole* and in light of Christ's coming.

2. All this means that the Christian faith is not a religion of the book (see *Catechism of the Catholic Church*, no. 108, and the 2008 Post-Synodal Apostolic Exhortation *Verbum Domini*). Sacred Scripture speaks only in the living community of the Church. There is a twofold exchange here, a relation of subordination and superiority. On the one hand, the Church is clearly subordinate to the Word of God, since she must always allow herself to be guided and judged by it; on the other hand, though, Scripture, in terms of its totality, can be interpreted adequately only in the living Church.

This position, adopted by the whole Church until the sixteenth century, was rejected in the Reformation with the principle of *sola Scriptura*. Christianity appears now as a religion of the book. In practice, however—because of the particular character of the Christian Bible, which we spoke about previously with the distinction between Old and New Testament, and because of the inherent "relativization" of the individual texts in it, which can be understood and traced back to a divine origin only in relation to the whole—the principle of Scripture is not applied in an absolutely rigid way. Adolf von Harnack expressed that concept in these terms: "The Old Testament is valid only relatively, standing beside the New.... With regard to the Bible, the absolute idolatry of the letter [*Grammatolatrie*] is not at all possible.... Biblicism received its salutary correction in the authority of the *apostolic teaching*, which, set alongside 'Scripture', organizes and delimits its authority." At the request of Erik Peterson for a further clarification in this regard, Harnack replied that "the so-called 'formal principle' of traditional Protestantism is a critical impossibility."[1] However

---

[1] Adolf von Harnack, "Das Alte Testament in den Paulinischen Briefen und in den Paulinischen Gemeinden", in *Sitzungsberichte der Preussischen Akademie der Wissenschaften* (Berlin: Preussischen Akademie der Wissenschaften, 1928), 141; Erik Peterson, *Theologische Traktate* (Munich: Kösel Verlag, 1951), 295.

one may judge in its specific details this formulation by the great Protestant theologian, it is still clear that, even to the Protestant way of thinking, the letter of the Bible simply does not stand on its own feet.

Anyone who considers these structural differences will guard against hasty parallels.

MUSIC AND LITURGY

Your Eminence! Your Excellencies! Distinguished professors! Ladies and gentlemen!

At this moment I can only express my most cordial thanks for the honor that you have granted me in conferring on me the *doctoratus honoris causa* [honorary doctorate]. I thank the Grand Chancellor, His dear Eminence Stanisław Cardinal Dziwisz, and the academic faculty of both universities. I am glad especially because in this way my bond with Poland, with Kraków, with the fatherland of our great Saint John Paul II has become even deeper. Because without him, my spiritual and theological journey is not even imaginable. With his living example, he also showed us how the joy of great sacred music can go hand in hand with the duty of common participation in the Sacred Liturgy, solemn joy with the simplicity of a humble celebration of the faith.

In the years of the postconciliar period, a very old conflict on this point had manifested itself with renewed passion. I myself grew up in the Salzburg region, which is marked by the great tradition of that city. There it was self-evident that festive Masses accompanied by choir and orchestra were an integral part of our experience of the faith in the celebration of the liturgy. It remains indelibly imprinted on my memory how, for example, no

Speech by Benedict XVI expressing his gratitude for the conferral of an honorary doctorate degree by the Pontifical University of John Paul II in Kraków and the Kraków Academy of Music. Castelgandolfo, July 4, 2015.

sooner did the first notes of the *Coronation Mass* by Mozart resound than the heavens opened, so to speak, and I experienced very profoundly the presence of the Lord. Already present alongside this, however, was also the new reality of the liturgical movement, especially through one of our chaplains who later became vice-rector and then rector of the Major Seminary in Freising. During my studies in Munich, then, very concretely I entered more and more into the spirit of the liturgical movement through the lectures of Professor Joseph Pascher, one of the most important experts of the council on liturgical matters, and above all through the liturgical life in the seminary community. Thus, little by little, the tension became perceptible between the *participatio actuosa* [active participation] in the liturgy recommended by the council and the solemn music that surrounded the sacred action, even though I did not yet feel it that strongly.

Vatican Council II wrote very clearly in its Constitution on the liturgy: "The treasure of sacred music is to be preserved and fostered with great care" (SC 114). On the other hand, the text underlines that the *participatio actuosa* of all the faithful in the sacred action is a fundamental liturgical category. In the constitution, these two imperatives still stand together peacefully, one after the other; in the reception of the council, they were often in a relation of dramatic tension. Influential circles of the liturgical movement maintained that in the future there would be room for the great choral works and certainly for orchestral Mass settings only in the concert halls, not in the liturgy. Here there could be a place only for singing and the common prayer of the faithful. On the other hand, there was dismay over the cultural impoverishment of the Church that would necessarily ensue. How could the two things be reconciled? How could the council be implemented in its entirety? These were the questions that confronted me and many other Catholics, simple folk no less than persons who had theological training.

At this point it is perhaps fair to ask the basic question: What is music, in reality? Where does it come from, and what does it tend toward?

I think that we can identify three "places" from which music springs.

A first source of it is the experience of love. When man was seized by love, another dimension of being was opened up to him, a new greatness and breadth of reality. And it drove him also to express himself in a new way. Poetry, song, and music in general were born from this being-struck, by this opening up of a new dimension of life.

A second origin of music is the experience of sadness, being touched by death, by sorrow, and by the abysmal moments in human existence. In this case, too, new dimensions of reality are opened up, in the opposite direction, that can no longer find a response in speech alone.

Finally, the third place of origin of music is the encounter with the divine, which from the beginning is part of what defines the human. Even more so, this is where the Totally Other is present: the Totally Great One who stirs up in man new ways to express himself. Perhaps it is possible to say that in reality in the other two areas also— love and death—the one who touches us is the divine mystery, and, in this sense, being touched by God is what constitutes the origin of music as a whole. I find it moving to observe how, for example in the Psalms, not even song is enough for man any more, and all the instruments are called on. The hidden music of creation is reawakened, its mysterious language. With the Psalter, in which the two motifs of love and death figure, too, we find ourselves right at the origin of the music of the Church of God. One could say that the quality of music depends on the purity and the grandeur of the encounter with the divine, with the experience of love and of sorrow. The purer and truer that experience is, the purer and greater will be also the music that is born and develops from it.

At this point I would like to express a thought that in recent times has increasingly occupied me, as the various cultures and religions enter more and more into relation with each other. In the sphere of the various cultures and religions, great literature is present, along with great architecture, great painting, and great sculptures. And everywhere there is music, too. And, nevertheless, in no other cultural sphere is there music with a grandeur equal to that of the music born in the sphere of Christian faith: from Palestrina to Bach, to Handel, down to Mozart, Beethoven, and Bruckner. Western music is something unique, which has no equals in the other cultures. This should make us think.

Certainly, Western music far surpasses the religious and ecclesial sphere. And, nevertheless, it does find its deepest source in the liturgy, in the encounter with God. In Bach, for whom the glory of God is ultimately the purpose of all music, this is quite obvious. The great and pure response of Western music developed in the encounter with the God who, in the liturgy, makes himself present to us in Jesus Christ. That music, for me, is a proof of the truth of Christianity. Where a response develops in this way, the encounter with the truth has occurred, with the true Creator of the world. For this reason, great sacred music is a reality of theological rank and of permanent significance for the faith of all Christendom, even though it is not at all necessary for it to be performed always and everywhere. On the other hand, though, it is also clear that it cannot disappear from the liturgy and that its presence can be an altogether special way of participating in the sacred celebration, in the mystery of faith.

If we think of the liturgy celebrated by Saint John Paul II on every continent, we see in the liturgical event the whole breadth of the expressive possibilities of the faith; and we see also how the great music of the Western tradition is not foreign to the liturgy, but was born and grew from it and in this way helps again and again to give form to it. We do not know the future of our culture and of sacred music. But one thing is clear: where the encounter with the living God who comes to us in Christ really occurs, there too is born and grows anew the response whose beauty comes from the truth itself.

The activity of the two universities that are conferring this honorary doctorate degree on me is an essential contribution so that the great gift of music that comes from the tradition of the Christian faith may remain alive and may help to make sure that the creative force of the faith will not be extinguished in the future, either. For this you all have my heartfelt thanks, not only for the honor that you have granted me, but also for all the work that you are doing in the service of the beauty of the faith. May the Lord bless you all.

THEOLOGY OF THE LITURGY

Nihil Operi Dei praeponatur, let nothing be preferred before the Work of God. With these words, Saint Benedict, in his *Rule* (43.3), established the absolute priority of Divine Worship over every other duty of the monastic life. This maxim, even in the monastic life, did not turn out to be immediately obvious, because for the monks their work in agriculture and in learning was also an essential duty. Both in agriculture and also in handicrafts and in the work of formation there could certainly be pressing temporal matters that might appear to be more important than the liturgy. Faced with all this, Benedict, in assigning priority to the liturgy, unequivocally highlights the priority of God himself in our life: "At the hour of Divine Office, as soon as the signal has been heard, let the monk leave whatever he may have in hand and make great haste, but with due gravity" (43.1).

In the consciousness of people nowadays, the things of God and, consequently, the liturgy do not appear urgent at all. Every possible thing has its urgency. God's cause seems never to be urgent. Now, it could be argued that monastic life is in any case something different from the life of men and women in the world, and this is of course right. And yet the priority of God that we have forgotten is true for everyone. If God is no longer important, the criteria for

Preface to the Russian-language edition of vol. XI, *Theology of the Liturgy*, of the *Collected Works* of Joseph Ratzinger—Benedict XVI. The text was completed on July 11, 2015, the Feast of Saint Benedict.

deciding what is important shift. In setting God aside, man subjects himself to constraints that make him the slave of material forces and that thus are opposed to his dignity.

In the years following the Second Vatican Council, I became conscious once again of the priority of God and of the Divine Liturgy. The misunderstanding of the liturgical reform that spread widely in the Catholic Church led to an increasing prominence of the aspect of instruction and of one's own activity and creativity. The doings of men almost made us forget the presence of God. In such a situation, it became increasingly clear that the existence of the Church is vitally dependent on the correct celebration of the liturgy and that the Church is in danger when the primacy of God no longer appears in the liturgy and thus in life. The most profound reason for the crisis that upset the Church lies in the eclipse of God's priority in the liturgy. All this led me to dedicate myself to the theme of the liturgy more extensively than in the past, because I knew that the true renewal of the liturgy is a fundamental prerequisite for the renewal of the Church. The studies that are collected in the present volume XI of the *Collected Writings* originated on the basis of this conviction. But fundamentally, even with all the differences, the essence of the liturgy is one and the same in the East and the West. And so I hope that this book may help the Christians of Russia also to understand in a new and better way the great gift that is given to us in the Sacred Liturgy.

Chapter Three

JEWS AND CHRISTIANS
IN DIALOGUE

GRACE AND VOCATION
WITHOUT REMORSE

Comments on the Treatise *De Iudaeis*

1. The Theological Significance of the Dialogue between Jews and Christians

Since Auschwitz, it has been clear that the Church needs to reflect on the question of the nature of Judaism. With the Declaration *Nostra aetate*, the Second Vatican Council provided the first basic directions. To be sure, we first have to specify what the treatise on the Jews is about. The celebrated book by Franz Mussner[1] on this theme is essentially a study of the enduring positive meaning of the Old Testament. This is certainly very important, but it does not correspond to the theme *De Iudaeis*. For "Judaism" in the strict sense does not mean the Old Testament, which is essentially common to Jews and Christians. Rather, there are two responses in history to the destruction of the Temple and to the new radical dispersion of Israel: Judaism and Christianity. In reality, Israel had already experienced

"Grace and Vocation without Remorse: Comments on the Treatise *De Iudaeis*" was completed on October 26, 2017, and published in *Internationale Katholische Zeitschrift Communio* 47 (July–August 2018). In Italian, the article was published in Benedetto XVI in dialogue with Rabbi Arie Folger, *Ebrei e cristiani*, ed. Elio Guerriero (Cinisello Balsamo: San Paolo, 2019), 39–75.

[1] Franz Mussner, *Traktat über die Juden* (Munich: Kösel, 1979; new expanded edition 1988). English edition: *Tractate on the Jews: The Significance of Judaism for the Christian Faith*, trans. Leonard Swidler (Philadelphia: Fortress Press, 1984).

several times the situation of the destruction of the Temple and of dispersion. However, each time they were permitted to hope for a rebuilding of the Temple and for a return to the Promised Land. The concrete situation was different after the destruction of the Temple in the year A.D. 70 and, definitively, after the failure of the Bar Kokhba revolt. In the new situation, the destruction of the Temple and the diaspora of Israel had to be accepted at least for a very long time. Finally, in the subsequent developments, it became increasingly clear that the Temple with its worship could no longer be restored, even if the political situation might allow it. Moreover, for the Jews there was the additional fact that there was another response to the destruction and scattering, a response that from the beginning considered all this as definitive and presupposed that the situation that had just been created was an event that could be expected on the basis of the faith of Israel itself. This was the reaction of the Christians, who initially indeed were not yet completely separated from Judaism. On the contrary, they claimed to uphold the continuity of Israel in their faith. As we know, only a small part of Israel has been able to accept this response, while the great majority resisted it and had to find a different solution. Of course, the two ways were by no means clearly distinct from one another at the beginning and continuously developed in their debate.

As the Acts of the Apostles shows, the community that arose in continuity with the message, the life, the death, and Cross of Jesus of Nazareth at first made its way entirely within Israel. Later on, however, it progressively expanded its proclamation in Greek societies and thus progressively came into conflict with Israel. The conclusion of Acts is indicative of this way of proceeding. According to this passage, in Rome, Paul began once again with the Jews, trying to win them over with an explanation of the Jesus event in the light of Scripture. He met with rejection, however, that he found foretold in Isaiah 6:9–10. Although, on the one hand, it seems to us that the division between the two communities is complete here, the process surely dragged on much longer elsewhere, so that the dialogue continued and now as before the two sides remained in debate with each other.

The Christian community expressed its identity in the writings of the New Testament, which originated essentially in the second half of the first century. However, it took some time before these writings coalesced into a canon, which then represents the authoritative document for Christian identity. These writings, however, do not stand on their own but constantly refer to the "Old Testament", that is, to the Bible of Israel. Their purpose is to show the authentic explanation of the Old Testament writings in the events relating to Jesus Christ. The Christian canon, then, by its nature consists of two parts: the Old Testament—the Scripture of Israel and now of Judaism—and the New Testament, which authentically elucidates the way to explain the Old in terms of Jesus. The Old Testament writings thus remain common to both communities, even though they are interpreted differently by the two groups. Moreover, among Christians the Greek translation of the Old Testament books that was made approximately from the third century B.C. on, the so-called Septuagint, was in practice recognized as canonical alongside and with the Hebrew Bible. In this way, the canon of the Christians was more extensive than that of the Jews. Moreover, there are some not entirely insignificant discrepancies between the text of the Septuagint and the Hebrew text. During this time of gradual mutual exclusion, Judaism for its part gave to the Hebrew text its definitive form. Furthermore, in the first centuries after Christ, in the Mishna and the

Talmud, it decisively formulated its own way of reading Sacred Scripture. All this, however, does not change the fact that one sacred book is common to both sides.

In the second half of the second century, however, Marcion and his movement tried to break this unity, so that Judaism and Christianity would become two opposing religions. With this aim in mind, Marcion created a canon that was in stark contrast to the Bible of Israel. In this view, the God of Israel (Old Testament) and the God of Jesus Christ (New Testament) are two different and opposing deities. For Marcion, the God of the Old Testament is a God of justice without grace; conversely, the God of Jesus Christ is a God of mercy and love. Accordingly, he formed a canon of the New Testament made up solely of the Gospel of Luke and ten of Paul's letters. Of course these writings had to be revised to serve his predetermined purpose. After a short period of activity, Marcion was excommunicated by the Church in Rome, and his religion was excluded as not belonging to Christianity. Of course, the Marcionite temptation still persists and reappears in certain situations in the history of the Church.

At this point, we note that Judaism and Christianity developed along divergent paths through a difficult process and took form in two different communities. And yet, despite the authoritative writings in which the identity proper to each is formulated, they remain connected through the common foundation of the "Old Testament" as their common Bible.

At this point, the question arises as to how the two communities, divided and yet united by a common Bible, judge one another. This is the origin of the treatise *De Iudaeis*, which is often called *Adversus Judaeos* and had a polemical purpose. The negative judgments about the Jews, which also reflect the political and social problems of coexistence, are well known and have repeatedly led to attacks against the Jews. On the other hand, as we saw earlier, with its rejection of Marcion in the second century, the Church of Rome made it clear that Christians and Jews worship the same God. The sacred books of Israel are also the sacred books of Christendom. The faith of Abraham is also the faith of the Christians; for them, too, Abraham is "the father of faith".

This fundamental commonality includes, of course, conflicting interpretations:

1. For Jews it is clear that Jesus is not the Messiah and therefore Christians are wrong to invoke their Bible, the "Old Testament". Their main argument is that the Messiah brings peace, whereas Christ did not bring peace into the world.

2. Christians respond with the argument that after the destruction of the Temple in A.D. 70 and in view of Israel's diaspora situation (which had no end in sight), Scripture, the "Old Testament", had to be reinterpreted; in its existing form, it could no longer be lived and understood. In his saying about the Temple being destroyed and rebuilt in three days, Jesus had foreseen the event of the destruction of the Temple and announced a new form of divine worship, which was to be centered on the offering of his Body. In this way and at the same time, the Sinai covenant was brought to its definitive form and became the New Covenant. In this same way, however, the worship was extended to all believers, thus giving to the promise of land its definitive meaning.

It was therefore evident to Christians that the preaching of Jesus Christ, his death and Resurrection, signified the God-given turning point of time, and consequently the interpretation of the Sacred Scriptures in light of Jesus Christ was, so to speak, legitimized by God himself.

Traditionally, the Old Testament is subdivided into three
types of books: *Torah* (Law), *Nebiim* (Prophets), and *Ketu-
bim* (wisdom books and psalms). In Judaism, the emphasis
is entirely on the Torah; on the other hand, if we exclude
the Psalms, then the other books, especially those of the
prophets, are relatively unimportant. The perspective for
Christians, however, is different. The whole Old Testament is now thought of as prophecy, as a *sacramentum futuri.*
Even the five books of Moses are essentially prophecies.
This entails a dynamic approach to the Old Testament in
which the texts are not to be read statically in themselves,
but must be understood as part of the whole, as a movement forward toward Christ. In the Church's praxis, this
has resulted in a concrete redistribution of emphasis: the
wisdom books are the foundation of moral teaching in
the catechumenate and for Christian life in general. The
Torah and the prophets are to be read as anticipated Chris-
tology. Finally, the Psalms are the great prayer book of the
Church. Traditionally, David is considered their author.
For Christians, however, Jesus Christ is the true David and
thus also the one who truly prays the Psalms. We read the
Psalms in terms of him and with him. The original historical meaning of the texts does not have to be repealed
thereby, but it is necessary to go farther. The first two lines
of the famous *Distychon* [couplet] on the four senses of
Scripture explain this progression: *Littera gesta docet. Quid
credas allegoria. Moralis quid agas. Quo tendas anagogia.*[2]
    With respect to this division, however, already by the
time of Gregory the Great we see a shift of emphases: allegory, the christological reading of all Scripture, loses some

---

[2] The literal sense teaches facts. The allegorical sense—what you should
believe. The moral sense—what you should do. The anagogical sense—the
destination to which you should travel. Cf. *Catechism of the Catholic Church,*
no. 118.

of its importance, while the moral sense comes increasingly to the fore. With Thomas Aquinas, who introduces a new view of theology, allegory is totally devalued (only the literal sense can be used in arguments), and in practice Aristotle's *Nicomachean Ethics* is put at the foundation of Christian morality. Then it becomes obvious that the entire Old Testament is in danger of losing its meaning.

2. The New Perspective on the Problems at Vatican II

Paragraph 4 of the Vatican II *Declaration on the Relation of the Church to Non-Christian Religions* is dedicated particularly to the relation between Christianity and Judaism. The errors of the past are rejected, and the truly authentic content of the Christian tradition in reference to Judaism is formulated. This establishes a valid criterion for a brand-new composition of the treatise *De Judaeis*. In 2015, the Commission for Religious Relations with the Jews published "A Reflection on Theological Questions Pertaining to Catholic-Jewish Relations on the Occasion of the 50th Anniversary of *Nostra aetate* (No. 4)" in which it offers an authoritative summary of the developments to date. From this overview, we can indeed say that the new, postconciliar view of Judaism can be summarized in two statements:

1. The "theory of substitution", which had hitherto dominated theological reflection in this field, should be rejected. It maintains that after rejecting Jesus Christ, Israel had ceased to be the bearer of God's promises, so that it can now be called the people "who for such a long time had been your chosen people" (*Prayer for the Consecration of the Human Race to the Sacred Heart of Jesus*).[3]

---

[3] Leo XIII, June 11, 1899.

2. Instead, it is more correct to speak of the covenant that was never revoked—a theme that was developed after the council in connection with Romans 9–11.

Both statements are basically correct, but in many respects imprecise, and they must be elaborated further and critically.

First, it should be noted that there was no [Catholic] "theory of substitution" [or "supersessionism"] as such before the council: none of the three editions of the *Lexikon für Theologie und Kirche*[4] (LThK, edited respectively by Buchberger, Rahner, and Kasper) contains an entry "theory of substitution". It is also missing from Protestant lexicons such as the RGG.[5] The expression "theory of substitution" does occur, however, in the index of the Kasper edition of the LThK, in the entries on the "*Altes Testament II*" (Old Testament II) (Breuning), "*Israel III*" (Breuning), and "*Volk Gottes I*" (People of God I) (W. Kraus).

Just as a "theory of substitution" did not exist as such, neither was a uniform view elaborated of Israel's position in salvation history after Christ. It is, however, correct to maintain that because of passages such as the parable of the vineyard tenants (Mk 12:1–11) or of the wedding feast (Mt 22:1–14; Lk 14:15–24) to which those who were invited did not come and were then replaced by others, the idea of Israel's rejection largely dominated the concept of its function within the current history of salvation.

---

[4] *Lexikon für Theologie und Kirche* is a German-language Catholic encyclopedia published in three editions by the Herder publishing house in Freiburg im Breisgau.

[5] *Religion in Geschichte und Gegenwart* [Religion in history and in the present]. As in the case of the *Lexikon für Theologie und Kirche*, this is a German encyclopedia in six volumes; the first edition was published in the years 1909–1913. Currently there are four editions of this reference work. The last, in eight volumes, was published in the years 1998–2005. The very young theologian Joseph Ratzinger was invited to collaborate on the third edition (1957–1965).

On the other hand, it was clear that Israel, or more precisely Judaism, always kept its own function within the current history of salvation and did not disappear into the world of other religions. Above all, two considerations have always ruled out the idea that the Jewish people were totally cut off from the promise:

1. Israel is undeniably still the possessor of Sacred Scripture. It is true that 2 Corinthians says that in reading Scripture the heart of Israel is covered by a veil and that this veil will be taken away only through turning to Jesus Christ (2 Cor 3:15–16). Yet the fact remains that it preserves in its hand the Sacred Scriptures of divine revelation. The Fathers of the Church, such as Saint Augustine, emphasized that there must be an Israel that does not belong to the Church in order to bear witness to the authenticity of the Sacred Scriptures.

2. Not only does Saint Paul write that "all Israel must be saved", but also the Book of Revelation by Saint John sees two groups of the redeemed: 144,000 from the twelve tribes of Israel (which expresses in another language the same idea as what Paul meant by the phrase "all Israel") and, next to them, "a great multitude which no man could number" (Rev 7:9) as the representation of those Gentiles who are saved. From the perspective of the New Testament tradition, this eschatological view is not a reality that will simply come to pass at the end, after many thousands of years; rather, the "eschatological" is something that in some way is always present.

From both perspectives, it was clear to the Church that Judaism did not become one religion among others, but is in a unique situation and therefore must be recognized as such by the Church, too. On this basis, the idea developed in the Middle Ages of the popes' twofold obligation to protect. On the one hand, they had to defend the

Christians against the Jews, but they also had to defend the Jews to the point where they alone [in the medieval world] could exist alongside Christians as a *religio licita*.

The question of substitution not only arises regarding Israel as such, but takes concrete form in the individual elements in which election appears: (1) the cultic legislation, which includes the Temple worship and also the major feasts of Israel; (2) the cultic laws concerning the individual Israelite: the Sabbath, circumcision, dietary precepts, regulations regarding purity; (3) the legal and moral teachings of the Torah; (4) the Messiah; (5) the promise of the land.

On the basis of this, we can then address also the subject of the covenant.

3. The Question of Substitution

We discuss, therefore, in the first section the essential elements of the promise, to which the concept of substitution could be applied; in the second section, we can then address the question of the covenant.

A. The Temple Worship

What does the denial of substitution mean for the Temple worship regulated in the Torah? Let us ask very concretely: Does the Eucharist take the place of the cultic sacrifices, or do they remain necessary in themselves? I think that here it becomes clear that the static view of law and promise that is behind an unqualified "no" to the "theory of substitution" must necessarily allow some exceptions. From the very beginning, the question of worship obviously developed in Israel in a dialectic between criticism of the cult and fidelity to the cultic regulations. In this regard I would like to cite chapter 3 of part 1 of my book *The Spirit of the*

Liturgy.[6] The part containing the cultic critique is found in passages such as 1 Samuel 15:22, Hosea 6:6, Amos 5:21–27, and so on. While in the Hellenistic realm, the criticism of the cult increasingly led to the total rejection of cultic sacrifice and took concrete form in the idea of a rational sacrifice [*Logos-Opfers*], in Israel the conviction always remains present that a merely spiritual sacrifice is not enough. I refer to two texts: Daniel 3:37–43 and Psalm 51:19ff.

Psalm 51 says clearly in verses 16–17: "You take no delight in [animal] sacrifice.... The sacrifice acceptable to God is a broken spirit [= contrite heart]." Then in verses 18–19, surprisingly, the prayer and the prediction follow: "Rebuild the walls of Jerusalem, then will you delight in right sacrifices, in burnt offerings and whole burnt offerings." Modern commentators tell us that, at this point, conservative elements reintroduced what the preceding verse had denied. In effect, there is a certain contradiction between the two groups of verses. But the fact that the last verse is indisputably part of the canonical text shows that a merely spiritual sacrifice alone is perceived as insufficient. The same conclusion follows from the aforementioned text from Daniel.

For Christians, the total sacrifice of Jesus on the Cross is the only possible and at the same time necessary synthesis of both views from God's perspective: the incarnate Lord gives himself entirely for us. His sacrifice includes the Body, the physical world in its full reality. But this is taken into the "I" of Jesus Christ and thus is completely elevated to the personal dimension. Thus for Christians it is clear that all previous worship finds its meaning and fulfillment only in the fact that it moves toward the sacrifice of Jesus

---

[6]Joseph Ratzinger, *The Spirit of the Liturgy*, trans. John Saward (San Francisco: Ignatius Press, 2000).

Christ. All previous worship always refers to it, and in it the whole system acquires meaning. In reality, therefore, there is no "substitution", strictly speaking, but a journey that eventually becomes one reality. And yet this entails the necessary disappearance of animal sacrifices, in place of which the Eucharist takes over ("substitutes").

Instead of the static view of substitution or nonsubstitution, this leads to a dynamic consideration of all salvation history, which in Christ finds its ἀνακεφαλαίωσις (recapitulation) (see Eph 1:10).

B. Cultic Laws concerning Individual Jews

Especially in the writings of Paul, the debate about the freedom of Christians from the Law has to do with the area of the cultic laws concerning individual persons (circumcision, the Sabbath, etc.). Today it is clear that, on the one hand, these ordinances were for the protection of Israel's identity in the great diaspora in the pagan world. On the other hand, the abolition of their binding character was the condition for the rise of worldwide Christianity among the Gentiles. From this perspective, these precise questions from the time of the separation of Israel and the Church no longer have any relevance for either side. There is no need to discuss further here the fact that from the sixteenth century on, in the interconfessional polemics, Protestants reproached Catholics for having reestablished the old legalism among Christians with their precepts for Sundays [Eucharistic fast] and Fridays [abstinence from meat], etc. (for having "substituted" new norms for the old ones).

C. Law and Morality

As for the moral precepts of the Torah, even among the Jews it is quite clear that, through the concrete development of the Law, so-called "casuistic law" offers models that are subject to development. Consequently there is no need for a debate between Christians and Jews on this point.

On the other hand, as for true moral teaching, properly speaking, which found its fundamental expression in the Decalogue, what the Lord says after the Sermon on the Mount in Matthew 5:17–20 applies: the Law remains valid, even if it must be read anew in new situations. This new reading, however, is neither a repeal nor a substitution, but rather a deeper understanding of its unaltered validity. Really there is no substitution here.

It is strange, though, that in the present situation many people even today claim a substitution precisely at this point: the eight beatitudes supposedly took the place of the commandments; the Sermon on the Mount is taken as a substitute for Old Testament morality in its entirety. On this entire question, allow me to refer to chapter 4 of volume I of my book *Jesus of Nazareth* (64–127).[7] A misunderstood Paulinism is the reason for the misunderstanding that a radical substitution occurred in this regard in fundamental teaching about Christian life. In reality, though, even in Paul's writings it is quite clear that the moral teaching of the Old Covenant, summarized in the twofold commandment of love, remains valid for Christians, albeit in the new context of love for Jesus Christ and being loved by him. Here the points "Temple worship" and "Law and morality" coincide in Paul, and this is the true Christian novelty: the crucified Christ bore every one of our sins. In Israel, the Day of Atonement and the daily sin offering were decreed to take and eliminate all the injustice in the world. Animal sacrifices, however, could only be a gesture that anticipated the true act of reconciliation.

[7] Joseph Ratzinger/Benedict XVI, *Jesus of Nazareth: From the Baptism in the Jordan to the Transfiguration*, trans. Adrian J. Walker (New York: Doubleday, 2007), 64–127.

The Son of God who takes upon himself all the sorrow and suffering of the world is now the true power of reconciliation. For the Christian, to be united with his death in baptism means to be surrounded by the forgiving love of God. It does not mean, however, that one's own life is now irrelevant or that the moral teaching no longer exists for him. Rather, it means that this moral teaching can and must be lived out anew in this being united with Christ in spiritual freedom.

Of course, the controversy over Pauline Christianity will continue, but I think that there should be a new clarity about the fact that the moral teaching in the Old and in the New Testament is, in the final analysis, identical and that there can be no "substitution" here.

D. The Messiah

The question of the messianic identity of Jesus is and remains the real contested question between Jews and Christians. Even though, being disputed, it will not cease to imply the separation of the two paths, recent research in the Old Testament has opened up new possibilities for dialogue. Developments in recent exegesis involving the re-dating and reinterpretation of Israel's great words of hope (Gen 49:10; Num 24:17; Sam 7:12–16; Ps 89:20–46; Amos 9:14f.; Is 7:10–17, 9:1–6, 11:1–9; Mic 5:1–5; Hag 2:20–23; Zech 4:8–14; and many psalm verses) show the polyphonic and multiform character of the hope in which the predominantly political figure of the new David—the "Messiah-king"—is only one form of hope among others. It is true that the entire Old Testament is a book of hope. At the same time, however, this hope expresses itself in many forms. Furthermore, it is true that this hope points less and less to an earthly and political power and that the importance of the Passion as an essential element of hope comes increasingly to the fore.

From the New Testament testimonies about Jesus, it is clear that he was wary of the title "Messiah" and of the ideas generally associated with it. This becomes apparent, for example, in Jesus' remark concerning the Davidic sonship of the Christ based on Psalm 110. Jesus recalls that the scribes portray the Messiah as the son of David. In the psalm, however, the Messiah appears, not as David's son, but as his Lord (Mk 12:35f.). But even when the title Christ is applied to Jesus by the disciples as their faith takes form, he immediately supplements and corrects the ideas hidden in this title with a catechesis on the suffering of the Savior (see Mk 8:27–33; Mt 16:13–23). Jesus, in his proclamation, personally associated himself, not with the Davidic tradition, but rather mainly with the promising figure of the son of man formulated by Daniel. Otherwise, what was central for him was the idea of the Passion, vicarious suffering and death, and atonement. The idea of God's suffering servant, of salvation through suffering, was essential for him: the songs of the suffering servant in Isaiah, as well as Zechariah's mysterious visions of suffering, define his image of the savior. These texts express Israel's experiences of faith during the times of exile and Hellenistic persecution. They appear as essential stages in God's journey with his people, which lead toward Jesus of Nazareth. But even Moses, who intervenes on behalf of his people and offers his own vicarious death, appears to shed light on the mission of Jesus Christ.

In his important study entitled *God's Self-Abasement in the Theology of the Rabbis*,[8] Peter Kuhn showed that the idea

---

[8] Peter Kuhn, *Gottes Selbsterniedrigung in der Theologie der Rabbinen* (Munich: Kösel Verlag, 1968), 13, text 1.

of God's self-abasement, and even suffering, is not foreign to Judaism and that there are significant approaches toward the Christian interpretation of hope in the Old Testament, even though final differences remain, of course.

In the medieval debates between Jews and Christians, it was common for the Jewish side to quote Isaiah 2:2–5 (Mic 4:1–5) as the core of the messianic hope. Anyone who made a messianic claim had to prove his identity in terms of these words: "He shall judge between the nations … and they shall beat their swords into plowshares, and their spears into pruning hooks; nation shall not lift up sword against nation, neither shall they learn war any more" (Is 2:4; Mic 4:3). It is clear that these words have not been fulfilled, but remain a future expectation.

In fact, Jesus read the promises of Israel within a broader understanding, in which the Passion of God in this world, and thus the suffering of the righteous one, becomes ever more central. A triumphant accent does not dominate at all, even in his images of the kingdom of God; they, too, are characterized by God's struggle for humanity and with humanity. In these days the weeds grow together with the wheat in the field of God's kingdom and are not torn up. Good and bad fish are found in God's net. The leaven of God's kingdom pervades the world from within only slowly so as to transform it. In conversation with Jesus, the disciples on the road to Emmaus learn that the Cross is precisely what must be the true center of the figure of the Messiah. The Messiah does not appear to be thought of primarily in terms of the royal figure of David.

The Gospel of John, as a concluding summary of Jesus' dialogue with the Jews (which at the same time mirrors the future dialogue between Jews and Christians), repositioned elsewhere the center of the figure of Jesus and, thus, of the interpretation of Israel's hopes. For John, the central statement about the promised figure is found in connection with the figure of Moses: "The LORD your God will raise up for you a prophet like me from among you, from your brethren—him you shall heed" (Deut 18:15). Another decisive feature for the figure of Moses is the fact that he "knew the LORD face to face". Deuteronomy itself notes in this regard that the promise had so far remained unfulfilled and that "there has not arisen a prophet since in Israel like Moses, whom the LORD knew face to face" (Deut 34:10). In the first chapter of his Gospel, John states programmatically that these still expectant words are now fulfilled in Jesus: "No one has ever seen God; the only-begotten Son, who is in the bosom of the Father, he has made him known" (Jn 1:18, cf. 13:25). To begin with, therefore, we can say that Jesus did not want to bring the new world of peace immediately, as prophesied in Isaiah 2 and Micah 4. Rather, he intended to show God to man (also to the Gentiles), and to them he revealed his will, which is the true salvation of man.

In my analysis of the eschatological discourse of Jesus in volume 2 of *Jesus of Nazareth*,[9] I showed that according to Jesus' view of history, a "time of the Gentiles" will come between the destruction of the Temple and the end of the world. At first, of course, it was thought to be of very short duration and yet essential as a part of the history of God with mankind.[10] Although this period of God's dealings with the world cannot be proved directly by the texts of the Old Testament, it does correspond to the unfolding of Israel's hope. This becomes increasingly clear in more recent times (Deutero-Isaiah, Zechariah).

[9] Joseph Ratzinger/Benedict XVI, *Jesus of Nazareth: Holy Week: From the Entrance into Jerusalem to the Resurrection*, trans. Philip J. Whitmore (San Francisco: Ignatius Press, 2011), 24–52.

.   [10] Ibid., 45–49.

Saint Luke tells us that the Risen Jesus, in the company of two disciples on the road to Emmaus, simultaneously guided them on an interior journey. At the same time, he rereads the Old Testament with them. In this way, they learn to understand in an entirely new way the promises and hopes of Israel and the figure of the Messiah. Thus they discover that the destiny of the Crucified and Risen One, who is mysteriously traveling with the disciples, is foreshadowed in these books. They learn a new reading of the Old Testament. This text describes the formation of the Christian faith in the first and second centuries and thus describes a path that should always be sought out and traveled. It fundamentally describes also the conversation between Jews and Christians as it was supposed to develop down to this day and unfortunately has been echoed, at least, only in rare moments.

The Fathers of the Church were fully aware of this new subdivision of history when, for example, they described the movement of history according to the threefold scheme of *umbra—imago—veritas* [shadow—image—truth]. The time of the Church (the "time of the Gentiles") has not yet arrived at the plain truth (= Is 2 and Mic 4). It is still *imago*; that is, a continuance in a transitory state, albeit in a new openness. Bernard of Clairvaux correctly expounded this state of affairs when he transformed the twofold advent of Christ into a threefold presence of the Lord and defined the time of the Church an *Adventus medius*.[11]

In summary, we can say that the whole story of Jesus, as the New Testament records it—from the account of the temptations to the story of Emmaus—shows that the time of Jesus, the "time of the Gentiles", is not the time of a cosmic transformation in which the final decisions

---

[11] An "intermediary coming." Ibid., 290–91.

between God and man are already made, but rather a time of freedom. In this time, God encounters man through the crucified love of Jesus Christ in order to gather them in a free Yes to the kingdom of God. It is the time of freedom, which also means a time in which evil still has power. God's power throughout this time is also a power of patience and of love, against which the power of evil is still active. It is a time of God's patience, which to us seems exaggeratedly excessive—a time of the victory of love and truth but also a time of their defeats. The ancient Church summed up the essence of this time in the saying "Regnavit a ligno Deus" (God reigned from a tree).

In journeying with Jesus like the Emmaus disciples, the Church learns to read the Old Testament with him and thus to understand it in a new way. She learns to recognize that this is precisely what was predicted about the "Messiah", and in the dialogue with the Jews she must continually seek to show that all this happens "according to the Scriptures". For this reason, spiritual theology has always emphasized that the time of the Church does not mean, for example, having arrived in paradise, but for the whole world corresponds to the forty years of Israel's exodus. It is the path of those who are liberated. In the wilderness, Israel was repeatedly reminded that its wandering was the result of its liberation from the bondage of Egypt; wayfaring Israel constantly wished to return to Egypt, failing to recognize the good of freedom as a good. The same is true of Christianity on its Exodus journey: again and again, it becomes difficult for men to recognize the mystery of liberation and freedom as a gift of redemption, and they desire to return to the condition before their liberation. Through the mercies of God, nevertheless, they can also learn constantly that freedom is the great gift that leads to true life.

E. The Promise of the Land

The promise of the land is reserved specifically for the children of Abraham as a historical people. Christians understand themselves as true descendants of Abraham (as incisively stated especially in the Letter to the Galatians), but not as a people in the earthly-historical sense. Given that they are a people among other nations, they expect no predetermined territory in this world. The Letter to the Hebrews explicitly set forth this view of the promise of land: "By faith [Abraham] sojourned in the land of promise, as in a foreign land, living in tents with Isaac and Jacob, heirs with him" of the same promise. For he looked forward to the city ... whose builder and maker is God" (Heb 11:9–10). "These all died in faith, not having received what was promised, but having seen it and greeted it from afar, and having acknowledged that they were strangers and exiles on the earth" (Heb 11:13). The *Letter to Diognetus* further elaborated this way of looking at it: Christians live in their respective countries as responsible citizens. At the same time, they know that their true city, their true country to which they are headed, is yet to come. The promise of land refers to the future world and relativizes the various affiliations to particular countries. The dialectic between belonging responsibly to this world and at the same time being on a journey defines the Christian understanding of country and nationality. Of course, this dialectic must always be worked through, suffered, and experienced anew.

On the other hand, Judaism adhered to the idea of the concrete descent from Abraham and thus had to search again and again, in a way necessarily, for a concrete inner-worldly meaning for the promise of land.

The failure of the Bar Kokhba revolt (A.D.132–135), which was theologically supported by parts of the rabbinate, meant of course for a long time a renunciation of such forms of political messianism. On the other hand, Maimonides (1135–1204) introduced a new approach in that he sought to extrapolate the expectation of land from the field of theology, giving it a rational form instead. However, a concrete reality did not emerge until the nineteenth century. The suffering of the large Jewish minority in Galicia and throughout the Middle East became the starting point for Theodor Herzl to found Zionism, which aimed to give a homeland again to the poor, suffering, displaced Jews. The events of the Shoah [Holocaust] made even more urgent the requirement of a state of their own for the Jews. In the disintegrating Ottoman Empire, to which the Holy Land belonged, it had to be possible to make the historical towns of the Jews a homeland for them once again. At the same time, the distance between interior motivations and concrete prospects was very great. A majority of Zionists were unbelievers, and they sought to make the territory a homeland for the Jewish people based on secularist premises. In Zionism, however, religious forces were always at work, and often, to the surprise of the agnostic parents, a turn to religion has come to pass in the new generation.

The question of how to evaluate the Zionist project was controversial within the Catholic Church, also. From the beginning, however, the dominant position was that the occupation of the territory understood theologically as a new political messianism was unacceptable. After the establishment of the state of Israel in 1948, a theological doctrine developed that eventually led to the political recognition of the state of Israel by the Vatican. This recognition is founded on the conviction that a state understood in a strictly theological sense—a Jewish religious state that wanted to be considered the political and religious fulfillment of the promises—is historically unthinkable according to the Christian faith and would be contrary to the Christian understanding of the promises. At the same time, however, it became clear that the Jewish people, like every other people, have a right to their own land on the basis of the natural law. As was just mentioned, it seemed obvious that the place for this purpose should be found in the territory of the historical dwelling place of the Jewish people. In the political situation of the disintegrating Ottoman Empire and the British protectorate, this could in fact be found according to the criteria of international law. In this sense, the Vatican recognized the state of Israel as a modern constitutional state and sees it as a legitimate homeland of the Jewish people. The rationale for its origin, however, cannot be derived directly from Sacred Scripture, and yet in a broader sense it may be the expression of God's fidelity to the people of Israel.

The non-theological character of the Jewish state means, however, that it cannot be considered the fulfillment of the promises of Scripture as such. Rather, the course of history shows a growth and unfolding of the promises, as we have seen with regard to the other dimensions of the promises also. Already in the first diaspora under King Nebuchadnezzar, God's love for his people was at work in the midst of judgment and gave a new, positive meaning to the diaspora. Only during the Exile did Israel's image of God, monotheism, become fully developed. According to the criteria of the time, indeed, a god who could not defend his country was no longer a god. Faced with the ridicule of the other nations, who scorned the God of Israel as vanquished and landless, it became clear that this God's divinity was resplendent precisely in the fact that he gave away the land: he was not only God of a particular country, but rather the whole world belonged to him. He exercised dominion over it and could subdivide it as

he willed. Thus Israel, in exile, definitively recognized that
their God was the God of gods, who freely disposes of
history and nations.

The Hellenistic persecution of Judaism was based in
reality, to its way of thinking, on an enlightened image of
God, which in principle should be unifying for all educated
people, so that there was no longer room for the particu-
larity and the missionary claim of the God of Israel. Precisely in the confrontation between Greek polytheism and
the one God of heaven and the earth whom Israel served,
an unexpected devotion to the God of Israel came about
among the God-seeking people of antiquity. This found
concrete expression in the movement of "God-fearers"
who gathered around the synagogues. In my dissertation
People and House of God in the Writings of Augustine,[12] I tried
to explain this phenomenon in greater depth, relying on
the analyses of Saint Augustine. The core of the whole
matter can be expressed briefly as follows: Ancient thought
had finally arrived at an opposition between the deities
worshipped in various religions and the real structure of
the world. In this conflict, the deities of the religions had
to be rejected as unreal, while the real power that had created the world and pervaded it appeared to be irrelevant
from a religious perspective.

In this situation, the God of the Jews, who truly was
the primordial power that philosophy had discovered,
appeared at the same time as the religious force that
addresses the individual person and in which man can
encounter the divine. This coincidence of philosophical
thought and religious reality was something new and was
able to make religion a tenable reality even from a rational

---

[12] Joseph Ratzinger, *Volk und Haus Gottes bei Augustin* (Munich: Karl Zink,
1954; reprinted with a new preface, Sankt Ottilien: EOS-Verlag, 1992).

perspective. The only thing that stood in the way was the bond of God to a single people and its legal ordinances. If, as in Paul's preaching, this bond were loosened and thus the God of the Jews could be regarded by all as their God, then the reconciliation of faith and reason had been achieved (see also my short book *The God of Faith and the God of Philosophy*).[13]

In this way, the Jews opened the door to God precisely through their final scattering in the world. Their situation in the diaspora is not only and not primarily punitive, but rather signifies a mission.

4. The "Never-Revoked" Covenant

With all that has been said so far, we have commented on the first basic element of the new consensus between Christianity and Judaism as it is presented in the reflections published by the Commission for Religious Relations with the Jews. This first basic element says that the "theory of substitution" does not adequately describe the relationship between Judaism and Christianity. We studied this thesis in terms of the basic elements in which the election of Israel is chiefly expressed and came to the conclusion that the thesis goes in the right direction, but must be reconsidered in its details. Now, though, we must turn our attention to the second element of this new consensus, that is, to the discourse about the "never-revoked covenant".

The document of the Commission for Religious Relations with the Jews explains in no. 39 that the thesis that

---

[13] Joseph Ratzinger/Benedict XVI: *Der Gott des Glaubens und der Gott der Philosophen* (Munich: Kösel-Verlag, 1968). This text is an excerpt from the author's inaugural lecture. Cf. Ratzinger/Benedict XVI, *Introduction to Christianity*, trans. J. R. Foster (San Francisco: Ignatius Press, 2004), 137–50.

"the covenant that God made with his people Israel per-
dures and is never invalidated" is not contained in *Nostra
aetate* but was expressed for the first time by John Paul II
on November 17, 1980, in Mainz. Since then it has been
included in the *Catechism of the Catholic Church* (no. 121)
and therefore belongs in a certain sense to the doctrinal
structure of the Catholic Church today. As in the case of
[the rejection of] the theory of substitution, here too the
core of what is said should be regarded as correct, but in
its individual points nevertheless still needs to be clarified
and deepened in many ways. First of all, it should be established that the Letter to the Romans (9:4), in enumerating
the special gifts of Israel, speaks, not about a covenant,
but about covenants. In fact, it is a mistake if in our theology covenant is generally viewed only in the singular,
or else in the strict juxtaposition of Old (First) and New
Covenant. For the Old Testament, the "covenant" is a
dynamic reality that takes concrete form in a developing
series of covenants. Recall as its main forms the covenant
with Noah, the covenant with Abraham, the covenant with
Moses, the covenant with David, and finally, in multiple
forms, the promise of the New Covenant.

The prologue of the Gospel of Matthew and the infancy
narrative by Saint Luke begin again at the covenant with
David. Each Gospel shows in its own way how the covenant was broken by men and had therefore come to an
end, but, on the other hand, how God causes a shoot to
grow from the stump of Jesse, and thus the covenant is
resumed by God (Is 11:1). The Davidic dynasty fails, like
all worldly dynasties. And yet the promise is fulfilled: his
kingdom will have no end (Lk 1:33).

The Letter to the Galatians is important for our question: chapters 3 and 4 draw a comparison between the
Abrahamic covenant and the Mosaic covenant. They say

that the Abrahamic covenant was granted in a universal and unconditional way. They say about the Mosaic covenant, on the other hand, that it was promulgated 430 years later. It was limited and connected with the condition of fulfilling the Law. This also means that it can fail if the conditions are not fulfilled. It has an intermediate function, but it does not abrogate the definitive and universal character of the Abrahamic covenant. We find a new development of the theology of the covenant in the Letter to the Hebrews, which repeats the promise of the New Covenant (proclaimed in a particularly resounding way in Jeremiah 31) and compares it with previous covenants. The Letter gathers them all together under the comprehensive title of the "first covenant", which now must be taken over [rilevata] by the "new", definitive covenant.

The theme of the New Covenant appears in several variations in Jeremiah, Ezekiel, Deutero-Isaiah, and Hosea. Particularly impressive is the description of the love story between God and Israel in chapter 16 of Ezekiel. God lovingly takes Israel unto himself in its time of her youth in the covenant that is meant to be definitive. Israel does not remain faithful and prostitutes herself with all kinds of deities. God's anger over this is not his last word. Instead, he takes Israel with him in a new and indestructible covenant. As for the "never-revoked covenant" that we are examining in greater depth here, it is correct that there is no revocation on God's part. Nevertheless, the actual history of God with Israel does include on man's part a breach of the covenant, the first form of which is described in the Book of Exodus. The long absence of Moses becomes for the people an occasion to give themselves a visible god, whom they adore: "The people sat down to eat and drink, and rose up to play" (Ex 32:6). Upon returning, "Moses saw that the people had broken loose" (Ex 32:25). Faced with the breaking of the covenant, Moses threw away the tablets that God himself had inscribed and broke them (Ex 32:19). God's mercy returned the tablets to Israel again, but they are always replacement tablets and at the same time warning signs that recall the breaking of the covenant.

What does that mean for the present question? The history of the covenant between God and Israel is, on the one hand, advanced indestructibly by God's election, but at the same time it is codetermined by the whole drama of human failure. Of course, given the infinite difference between the contracting parties, the word "covenant" cannot be understood in the sense of equal partners. The disparity between the two partners makes the covenant look more like the Oriental model as concessions granted by the great king. This is evident also in the linguistic form: the word *syntheke* (partnership) is not used, but rather *diatheke*. This is why the Letter to the Hebrews does not speak of "covenant" but rather of "testament". Accordingly, the Sacred Scriptures are called, not Old and New Covenant, but rather Old (first) and New Testament.

The whole journey of God with his people finally finds its summary and definitive form in the Last Supper of Jesus Christ, which anticipates and carries within itself the Cross and Resurrection. We do not need to dwell here on the complicated problems of the formation of the two textual traditions: Mark and Matthew, on the one hand, and Luke and Paul, on the other. In one case, the Sinai tradition is taken up. What happened there comes to definitive fulfillment here, and thus the promise of the New Covenant in Jeremiah 31 becomes present here. The Sinai covenant always was by its very nature a promise, a path to what is definitive. After all the times it was demolished, the love of God, which goes so far as the death of the Son, is itself the New Covenant.

Let us now try to come to a final judgment about the formula of the "never-revoked covenant". We first had to raise two linguistic objections. The word "revoke" is not part of the vocabulary of divine action. "Covenant", in the story of God's history with mankind described in the Bible, is not singular, but happens in stages. Now, beyond these formal objections, we must say critically with regard to content that this formula does not express the real drama of the story between God and man. Certainly, God's love is indestructible. But the history of the covenant between God and man also includes human failure, the breaking of the covenant, and its internal consequences: the destruction of the Temple, the scattering of Israel, and the call to repentance and its interior consequences that make man worthy of the covenant once again. The love of God cannot simply ignore man's No, which wounds God himself and, thus, man too. Although God's wrath and the severity of his punishments are described in the books of the prophets and also in the Torah, it is still necessary to keep in mind that God's punitive actions become a suffering for himself. It is not the end of his love, but a new stage of it.

I would like now to quote a single text that clearly illustrates this intertwining of anger and love and therein the definitiveness of love. After all the threats that had come before, the saving love of God appears in all its greatness in Hosea 11:7–9: "My people are bent on turning away from me; so they are appointed to the yoke, and none shall remove it. How can I give you up, O Ephraim! How can I hand you over, O Israel! ... My heart recoils within me, my compassion grows warm and tender. I will not execute my fierce anger, I will not again destroy Ephraim." Between the guilt of mankind and the threat of the final destruction of the covenant lies the suffering of God: "My heart recoils within me, ... for I am God and not man ... and I will not come to destroy." What is said here in a grandiose and moving way is realized in the words of Jesus Christ at the Last Supper when he gives himself to death and, thus, in the Resurrection inaugurates the New Covenant.

The Sinai covenant is transposed and reestablished in the New Covenant in the Body and Blood of Jesus—that is, in his love that goes beyond death—and this gives a new and permanently valid form to the covenant. Jesus thus responds in advance to the two historical events that shortly afterward would radically change the situation of Israel and the concrete form of the Sinai covenant: the destruction of the Temple, which proved to be increasingly irrevocable, and the scattering of Israel in a worldwide diaspora. Here we touch on the "essence" of Christianity and on the "essence" of Judaism, which for its part developed a response to these events in the Talmud and the Mishnah. How can the covenant be lived now? This is the question that has separated the concrete reality of the Old Testament into two paths, Judaism and Christianity.

The formula of the "never-revoked covenant" may have been helpful in an initial phase of the new dialogue between Jews and Christians. In the long run, however, it proves to be insufficient to express adequately enough the magnitude of the reality. If summary formulas are considered necessary, I would refer mainly to two expressions of Sacred Scripture in which the essential point is expressed. In reference to the Jews, Paul says: "the gifts and the call of God are irrevocable" (Rom 11:29). In reference to everyone, Scripture says, "if we endure, we shall also reign with him; if we deny him, he also will deny us; if we are faithless, he remains faithful—for he cannot deny himself" (2 Tim 2:12–13).

RABBI ARIE FOLGER RESPONDS TO "GRACE AND VOCATION WITHOUT REMORSE"

When Jewish and Catholic representatives gathered in Vienna on October 26, 2017, to celebrate the ceremonial handing over of the German edition of the rabbinic declaration *Between Jerusalem and Rome*, the ink was still drying on the final lines of a document written by Pope Emeritus Benedict XVI. The latter text has now appeared in the theological journal *Communio*—and it is making headlines.

In the public discourse on the matter, some are saying that the text goes against the spirit of the Declaration *Nostra aetate*, which by now is more than fifty years old, that it may represent a danger for Catholic-Jewish dialogue, and even that it lays the groundwork for a new kind of anti-Semitism on a Christian foundation. Is that right?

1. Claim to Salvation

The Jesuit theologian Christian Rutishauser finds the text disappointing in many respects. If its intention is "to defend Christ's universal claim to salvation against relativism", then it overshoots the mark, Rutishauser writes

In response to the *Communio* article by Pope Emeritus Benedict XVI, Arie Folger, the chief rabbi of Vienna, wrote an article entitled "Gefahr für den Dialog?" which was published in *Jüdische Allgemeine* on July 16, 2018. Translated from the original German by Chase Faucheux and Michael J. Miller.

in the *Neue Züricher Zeitung*. Only with a much more positive attitude toward living Judaism "can Jews and Christians live in an appreciative relationship and listen to one another on the basis of faith", Rutishauser says.

When I read the controversial text, I perceive it quite differently. I see a text that was written by an important, conservative Catholic theologian for the Vatican's internal use and therefore should not be measured by standards of public and interreligious discourse.

2. Declaration

And although Benedict does not mention our declaration, it is fairly self-evident that it played a significant role in his reflections. He finished writing his article a mere eight weeks after we visited the Vatican and presented the official text to his successor, Francis.

What does the papal text say? Benedict engages with the two major theses of the document *The Gifts and Calling of God are Irrevocable*, which was issued in 2015 by the Vatican Commission for Religious Relations with the Jews. Benedict takes a position on two theses: first, that the Church no longer understands herself as the new Israel that has been chosen instead of the now outcast Israel (as per the thesis that the Vatican now considers outdated), in other words, the so-called theory of substitution; second, that the Church now professes that God's covenant with the people of Israel is eternal and irrevocable.

3. Theses

In Benedict's view, the two theses need to be explored in greater depth and articulated more precisely in order to make sense from a Christian perspective. Regarding the theory of substitution, Benedict suggests it never existed. He sees in various New Testament sources confirmation for the idea that Jews will continue to exist as a separate community until the end of time. They occupy a special position in Christian theology; in particular, they are the custodians of the Hebrew Bible, which Christians continue to view as the Word of God and to which they are indebted.

Insofar as Jews and Christians interpret the Torah differently and live out its laws in different ways, this is to be attributed to different readings of the text and different theologies, but both groups consider it a text that they must accept. Since Benedict's Church has never accepted a theory of substitution, one can speak only of substitution in individual areas: for example, in the way that Christians believe that after the destruction of the Temple and the crucifixion of Jesus, the sacrificial laws acquired a new and (for Christians) higher meaning and would accordingly be lived out spiritually. For Jews, this reinterpretation is neither acceptable nor sensible; nor does it conform to *halakha*.

4. Revisionism

Benedict's thesis that the theory of substitution was never part of the Church's teaching is an instance of ahistorical revisionism that ignores the real suffering inflicted on Jews for centuries on account of the doctrine of *verus Israel*. In spite of all of Benedict's philosophical arguments, the sculpture of the *Synagoga* on the façade of Strasbourg Cathedral still depicts a miserable, blind woman, while on the other side stands the radiant *Ecclesia*. Nor have the "*Judensäue*" ("Jewish swine") of the German cathedrals suddenly disappeared.

The second thesis, which Benedict is able to explain in precise terms, says that the Church professes that God's covenant with the people of Israel is eternal and irrevocable and is particularly important for Christian-Jewish dialogue. The Vatican Commission cited this in its statement that "the Catholic Church neither conducts nor supports any specific institutional mission work directed toward Jews."[14]

In Benedict's opinion, this second claim "should be regarded as correct, but in its individual points nevertheless still needs to be clarified and deepened in many ways". This seems to suggest that, in his view, Jews, too, can attain salvation only thanks to Jesus.

5. Expectations

This has made various commentators quite upset, which I find difficult to understand. What do we expect from a pope? Do we Jews really expect the Church to accept Judaism as a legitimate way around the Church's teaching?

We do not need the Church's approval in order to believe in the truth of Judaism. For this we can trust in our ancestors, who passed down to us the Torah and the valid way of interpreting it in an unbroken chain from Sinai to the present day. We are not dependent on the Church to grant us salvation, nor does the Church have a right to demand

[14] Dicastery for Promoting Christian Unity, Commission for Religious Relations with the Jews, " 'The Gifts and the Calling of God Are Irrevocable' (Rom 11:29): A Reflection on Theological Questions Pertaining to Catholic-Jewish Relations on the Occasion of the 50th Anniversary of 'Nostra ætate' (No. 4)" (December 10, 2015), http://www.christianunity.va/content/unitacristiani/en /commissione-per-i-rapporti-religiosi-con-l-ebraismo/commissione-per-i -rapporti-religiosi-con-l-ebraismo-crre/documenti-della-commissione/en .html.

that we legitimize her way and grant salvation to her. We are two different, independent faith communities [*Konfessionen*]. And, nevertheless, we profess brotherhood with one another. Our interfaith work does not gloss over our differences; rather, we want to work together despite our fundamental differences.

Indeed, it is an important principle of interfaith dialogue that we recognize the autonomy of each other's faith communities and respect their boundaries.

6. Covenant

There are admittedly some Christian theologians, both Catholic and Protestant, who try to envision a dual covenant, whereby God made two separate covenants. According to this view, there is the one with the Jewish people, who—without faith in Jesus and without the New Testament—attain salvation by observing *halakha* in its entirety. Later the other covenant was made with Christians, mediated by the person and the teaching of Jesus. This, however, is not a mainstream view.

Note that even the most philo-Semitic statements of the Vatican mention only the covenant of Abraham and never the covenant of Moses or the covenant at Sinai. That God would leave the covenant of Abraham without a substitute to this day is something that many Christians find understandable; after all, despite the rejection of faith in Jesus, they can give as a good reason for a covenant the fact that we are related to him, and blood, as everyone knows, is thicker than water. An alternative covenant at Sinai would raise considerable theological problems for many Christians, not least because the core teachings of Christianity are not halachically acceptable.

7. Commission

Even the Vatican Commission has difficulty understanding the unrevoked Abrahamic covenant, which it described in 2015 as "an unfathomable divine mystery". Benedict is merely trying to shed some light on this mystery in the Vatican's thinking.

Benedict's suggestion that Christians should teach Jews how to understand the relevant passages in the Hebrew Bible christologically is nevertheless highly problematic. Does he mean to repudiate the papal commission's commitment no longer to pursue a mission to the Jews? For centuries Jews were forcibly proselytized. After so much Jewish blood that was spilled as a result of Christian hostility toward Jews, it should be clear to Benedict that there can be no positive outlook on the "mission to the Jews".

A third theme of Benedict's text that deserves our attention is the position of the Church with regard to Zionism. Benedict admits that the idea of the Jews returning to Zion was theologically untenable. This is why the Church tried for decades to ignore any religious meaning of the establishment of the state of Israel. To the Church, Israel was a country like all others, and the Vatican based its recognition of the state on the fact that Jews also were entitled to have a homeland. Indirectly, Benedict then acknowledges that this is a difficult position to maintain.

His remark that the Jewish state "cannot be considered the fulfillment of the promises of Scripture as such" indicates that he is aware that this theological devaluation of Zionism comes across as dishonest and unserious. Yes, it is time for the Church to realize that the return to Zion is religiously significant. While we Jews might quarrel among ourselves over *what* the religious significance of Zionism is, the fact that it *is* significant is certain even to the anti-Zionist Hasidic group Satmar.

8. Exile

As already mentioned, Benedict's text was intended as an internal Vatican document. For this reason, my next and last point is not a criticism, but still an important rejoinder: Contrary to all his other main points, where he also mentions the Jewish point of view, Benedict understands the most recent and longest Jewish exile exclusively from a Christian perspective. The long exile supposedly demonstrated that the hopes for the coming of the Messiah according to the Jewish idea and the rebuilding of Israel and of the Temple were unrealistic; likewise, according to this view, the promise of land is obsolete. No, Pope Emeritus Benedict, that is not how we perceive the reality at all!

In *Between Jerusalem and Rome*, we put it this way: "As God chose Avraham, and subsequently Yitzchak and Yaakov, He entrusted them with a dual mission: to found the nation of Israel that would inherit, settle, and establish a model society in the holy, promised land of Israel, all while serving as a source of light for all mankind.... After the darkest hour since the destruction of our holy Temple in Jerusalem, when six million of our brethren were viciously murdered and the embers of their bones were smoldering in the shadows of the Nazi crematoria, God's eternal covenant was once again manifest, as the remnants of Israel gathered their strength and enacted a miraculous reawakening of Jewish consciousness. Communities were reestablished throughout the Diaspora, and many Jews responded to the clarion call to return to Eretz

Yisrael, where a sovereign Jewish state arose."[15] This is what we understand by the promise that we will be a *mamlechet kohanim v'goy kadosh*—"a kingdom of priests and a holy nation" (2 Moses [= Ex] 19:6).

Chief Rabbi Arie Folger, M.B.A.
Jewish Community of Vienna
Vatican City, August 23, 2018

LETTER FROM BENEDICT XVI
TO RABBI ARIE FOLGER

To Rabbi Arie Folger
Chief Rabbi of the Jewish worship community in Vienna
Vatican City, August 23, 2018

Dear Rabbi Folger,

Professor Tück at the University of Vienna sent me your article "Dialogue in Danger?", and I must thank you cordially for this important and constructive contribution.

First of all, you clarified the genre to which my text belongs. It is a document that pertains to the theological dispute between Jews and Christians over the right understanding of God's promises to Israel. Christianity exists in the first place only because, after the destruction of the Temple and citing the life and death of Jesus of Nazareth, a community formed around Jesus. This community was convinced that the Hebrew Bible as a whole was about Jesus and had to be interpreted in reference to him. This conviction, however, was not shared by the majority of the Jewish people. Thus, the dispute arose as to whether one interpretation or the other was correct. Unfortunately, on the Christian side, this dispute was frequently,

Published in German as "Briefwechsel Benedikt XVI.—Rabbi Arie Folger", *Internationale Katholische Zeitschrift Communio* 47/6 (2018). The two letters were published in Italian in the volume *Ebrei e cristiani*, ed. Elio Guerriero (Cinisello Balsamo: San Paolo, 2019), 77–95. English trans. Chase Faucheux and Michael J. Miller.

or nearly always, conducted without due reverence to the other side. On the contrary, the sad history of Christian anti-Semitism developed, which ultimately led to the sad story of Nazi anti-Semitism, culminating in the woeful climax of Auschwitz.

Meanwhile, it is important to continue the dialogue between the two communities about the correct interpretation of the Bible of the Jewish people. Their faith, indeed, is based on this interpretation. One important methodological basis for this dialogue is the document of the Pontifical Biblical Commission "The Jewish People and Their Sacred Scripture in the Christian Bible", dated May 24, 2001, which I took as the methodological basis of my reflections. As far as is humanly foreseeable, this dialogue will never lead to the unity of the two interpretations within ongoing history. This unity is reserved to God at the end of history. In the meantime, the two sides have the task of confronting one another in order to understand properly, each side considering respectfully the views of the other. The central content of this dialogue will be God's great promises to Israel, which I summed up in my article with the following key expressions: the messianic hope of Israel, the land, the covenant, the moral instruction, and the correct worship of God. Allow me to mention briefly once again what I tried to say in my paper about the Christian understanding of these topics:

1. It stands to reason that the messianic promise will always be controversial. Nevertheless, I do believe that progress in mutual understanding is possible here. I sought to reexamine the entirety of the messianic promises in their many forms and thus to arrive at a new understanding of the "already" and the "not yet" at the inner core of this hope. The form of messianic expectation that is based on the figure of David remains valid but is limited in its

significance. As I see it, the definitive figure of hope is Moses, whom Scripture says spoke with the Lord face to face, as a man speaks to his friend. Jesus of Nazareth appears to us Christians as the central figure of hope, because he has an intimate, familiar relationship with God. From this new point of view, the time of the Church no longer appears as the time of a definitively redeemed world; rather, for Christians, the time of the Church is what the forty years in the desert were for Israel. Consequently, its essential content is the freedom of the children of God, the exercise of which is no less difficult for the "nations" than it was for Israel. If we accept this new understanding of the time of the Gentiles, then we have available a theology of history that the Jews cannot accept as such, but which might offer a new basis for common effort in fulfilling our task.

2. A suitable interpretation of the promise of land, in the context of the formation of the state of Israel, is of vital importance to all sides today. Without repeating all that I said in my text, I would like to reiterate my thesis, which is important not only for Christians, that the state of Israel as such cannot be regarded theologically as the fulfillment of God's promise of land. Rather, it is in itself a secular state, which of course quite legitimately has religious foundations. To the fathers of the state of Israel (Ben Gurion, Golda Meir et al.), it was quite clear that the state that they created had to be a secular state—if for no other reason than because that was the only way it could survive. I believe that the development of the idea of the secular state can also be largely attributed to Jewish thought, whereby "secular" does not mean "anti-religious". Only on this premise was the Holy See able to establish diplomatic relations with the state of Israel. And the dispute with the Arabs and also the search for peaceful coexistence with them are likewise connected

with this outlook. I think, furthermore, that in this way it is not difficult to see that in the formation of the state of Israel we can recognize in a mysterious way God's fidelity to Israel.

3. As for morality and worship, in my opinion we can recognize a greater affinity between Israel and the Church today than in the past. From the beginning of the modern era, the entire matter was overshadowed by the anti-Jewish thinking of Luther, for whom the rejection of the Law was fundamental following his Tower Experience. This experience, which had lifelong significance for him, became connected with the thinking of Marcion, resulting in a pseudo-religious Marcionism with which we have not yet really come to terms. It seems to me that this point in particular offers important opportunities for a renewed dialogue with Judaism.

Dear Rabbi Folger, I have gone on too long, and for this I beg your pardon.

Thank you again for your article.

Yours truly,
Benedict XVI

LETTER FROM RABBI ARIE FOLGER
TO BENEDICT XVI

Vienna, 24 Elul 5778—4 September 2018

His Holiness
Benedict XVI Joseph Ratzinger
Pope Emeritus

Your Eminence,

Thank you for your letter dated August 23, which I received on the 30th via email forwarded by Archbishop Georg Gänswein and Professor Jan-Heiner Tück.

I read with great interest your letter and the ideas contained in it. More than your article in *Communio*, which, as you and I agree in emphasizing, is an internal Christian document, your letter presents ideas that can indeed serve as a guide in the Christian-Jewish dialogue.

First and foremost, I would like to express my full agreement with your third point. It is quite true. Jews and Catholics in this time are called in particular to work together to uphold moral standards in the Western world. The West is becoming more and more secular—while a growing minority are once again taking their religion and their religious duties seriously—and lately the majority are becoming increasingly intolerant of religion, believers, and religious practices. For this reason we can and should take a public stand together more often. Together, we can be much stronger than we could separately.

Moreover, we share common values, and both faith communities treasure the Hebrew Bible. Even if we interpret many passages differently, we have a common foundation in it.

In addition, we both represent religious confessions that show great tolerance and support it politically. Of course, in each of these two faith communities there are also some extremists, but as a member of the Conference of European Rabbis, the Orthodox Rabbinical Conference of Germany, and the Rabbinical Council of America, all renowned Orthodox Jewish organizations, I can attest that we consider it very important to work for a tolerant society and that we are always appalled when a fanatic from among our own ranks speaks or behaves otherwise. I believe that the same is true of the Catholic Church. And therefore these religious representatives, such as our colleagues and ourselves, are precisely the ones who must commit themselves to work for a diverse and tolerant society in which believers and their concerns are fully respected, too, and religious convictions may make their contribution to the public debate.

As for your second point, I consider it an important topic for Jewish-Christian dialogue. As we implied in our document *Between Jerusalem and Rome*, we understand that it was significantly easier for the Church to establish diplomatic relations with a secular state of Israel. And certainly it seems easier to make compromises in favor of the Palestinians if the state considers itself to be secular. But you yourself write that even a secular state does not preclude the blessings of God and that it is a confirmation of the everlasting covenant with the Jewish people. This certainly reduces the distance between our respective positions.

Here I would like to emphasize that, as you write, the structure of the democratic state of Israel is certainly a temporal, secular structure. At the same time, though, I maintain that the religious perspective cannot be irrelevant, at least for the mass return to Zion of Jews from all over the world. Cardinal Koch, moreover, suggested in a letter (to us five rabbis who had sent an open letter to him) that we meet to discuss this topic, a suggestion that we will gladly accept. Indeed, we just composed a letter regarding this matter that will soon reach him. Should the opportunity arise, I would be very glad if we could meet for a private conversation in Rome.[16]

And I come now to your first point. As a student of several disciples of Rabbi Joseph Ber Soloveitchik, I find I have much greater sympathy with your third point (to work to promote the moral sensibilities of society, the better to protect believers and their religious freedom) than with the idea of theological dialogue, which Rav Soloveitchik tended to dismiss. Your invitation, nevertheless, strikes me as potentially more effective, because it proposes a more modest goal. You are not advocating the kind of dialogue in which we seek to persuade one another, but a dialogue in which we seek to understand each other better. I find particularly important your statement, "As far as is humanly foreseeable, this dialogue will never lead to the unity of the two interpretations within ongoing history. This unity is reserved to God at the end of history." Indeed, it signals that the dialogue should promote

---

[16] The private meeting that Rabbi Folger hoped for actually took place on January 16, 2019, at Mater Ecclesiae Monastery. Present at that meeting, besides Benedict XVI and Rabbi Folger, were Cardinal Koch, President of the Commission for Religious Relations with the Jews, Zsolt Balla, Rabbi of the State of Saxony and member of the governing board of the Orthodox Rabbinical Conference of Germany, and Josh Ahrens, Rabbi of the Jewish community in Darmstadt. After that meeting, Rabbi Folger wrote about Pope Benedict: "Truly he is no longer young, but still fully in control of himself intellectually. I found him to be a very sympathetic and profound thinker who is disgusted by anti-Semitism and anti-Judaism in all its forms." Cf. Benedetto XVI, *Ebrei e cristiani*, 16. (Editor's note.)

understanding and friendship, but does not aim to proselytize or to discuss theological points.

Allow me to revisit a theme from your *Communio* article, that of the unrevoked covenant. As I wrote in my article in the *Jüdische Allgemeine*, I fully understand that Christians want to remain true to the tenets of their faith. That is why the Pontifical Commission for Religious Relations with the Jews described this unrevoked covenant as a mystery. In your article you attempt to deal with the tension surrounding this mystery. Here I would like to emphasize, not surprisingly, how important this idea of the unrevoked covenant is in combating anti-Semitism. In the past century, some Christians justified a great deal of suffering inflicted on Jews precisely with the argument that the covenant had been revoked. Now, I would not presume to ask another faith community to interpret its doctrines in one way or another. However, because of the real suffering that has been inflicted on Jews by Christians in the past based on this reasoning, I must make an exception here and ask you to reaffirm the contrary thesis, namely, that of the unrevoked covenant, which is now held in high regard in the Church and which in your view should never have been considered otherwise.

In *Communio*, you maintain that the Church never believed in the theory of substitution. As the emeritus supreme representative of the Catholic Church, you are entitled to make that argument. In fact, it is very important to anchor these somewhat "new" views historically in the past and in the most ancient teachings of the Church. In this regard, however, the crimes of the past cannot be forgotten; even though they are now considered contrary to Christian principles, they were committed by Christians in the name of Christianity. Today the *Judensäue* [Jewish swine] on German church buildings and the statues of *Ecclesia* and

Synagoga on the façade of the Cathedral in Strasbourg (and of many other places) recall both a dark past and today's peaceful and friendly relations, and that is fine. What we cannot do, however, is forget history and claim that everything has in fact always gone well because the perpetrators presumably supported an erroneous theology. I dare not say that you are trying to whitewash history, no. God forbid! However it would mean a lot to us Jews if we could see, together with your second thesis that the Church could never maintain the thesis that it replaced the Jewish people, an acknowledgment also that in certain eras Christians nevertheless supported the theory of substitution—in other words, contrary to the authentic teaching of the Church— and in this way justified unspeakable suffering.

I continue to hope that our correspondence—and by "our" I mean also our respective colleagues—will help to strengthen and deepen our dialogue and that it will promote action on behalf of a better society.

In a few days we will be celebrating Rosh HaShanah,[17] which we consider to be, among other things, the anniversary of the creation of Adam and therefore a universal holiday for mankind. And so I wish you a *Shana tovah u'metuka*, a sweet and happy new year, for Jews, Christians, and all mankind.

Sincerely yours,
Arie Folger
Chief Rabbi of Vienna

[17] Rosh HaShanah is the holiday marking the beginning of the Jewish year. It is celebrated in the days between the end of September and the beginning of October. In 2019 it ran from Sunday, September 29, to Tuesday, October 1. (Editor's note.)

Chapter Four

TOPICS FROM DOGMATIC THEOLOGY

FAITH IS NOT AN IDEA,
BUT A LIFE

Your Holiness, the question posed this year as part of the symposium promoted by the rectorate of the Gesù (the residence for Jesuit seminarians in Rome) is that of justification by faith. The latest volume of your collected works (volume 4: Einführung in das Christentum *[Freiburg im Breisgau: Herder, 2014]) highlights your resolute affirmation: "The Christian faith is not an idea, but a life." Commenting on the famous Pauline affirmation in Romans 3:28, you mentioned, in this regard, a twofold transcendence: "Faith is a gift communicated through the community, which for its part is also a gift" (page 512). Could you explain what you meant by that statement, taking into account of course the fact that the aim of these days of study is to clarify pastoral theology and vivify the spiritual experience of the faithful?*

The question concerns what faith is and how one comes to believe. On the one hand, faith is a profoundly personal contact with God, which touches me in my innermost being and places me in front of the living God in absolute immediacy in such a way that I can speak with him, love him, and enter into communion with him. But at the same time this reality which is so fundamentally personal also inseparably pertains to the community. It is an essential

Interview granted to Jesuit Father Daniele Libanori for a symposium on justification by faith (Rome, rectorate of the Gesù, October 8–10, 2015). The text was published in *L'Osservatore Romano* (March 16, 2016), and an English translation appeared in the paper's weekly English edition on April 1, 2016, page 8. The translation has been slightly emended.

part of faith that I be introduced into the "we" of the children of God, into the pilgrim community of brothers and sisters. The encounter with God means also, at the same time, that I myself become open, torn from my closed solitude and received into the living community of the Church. That living community is also a mediator of my encounter with God, although that encounter touches my heart in an entirely personal way.

Faith comes from hearing, as Saint Paul teaches us. Listening, in turn, always implies a partner. Faith is not a product of reflection, and it is not an attempt to penetrate the depths of my own being. Both of these things may be present, but they remain insufficient without the "listening" through which God challenges me, from without, from a story he himself created. In order for me to believe, I need witnesses who have met God and make him accessible to me.

In my article on baptism, I spoke of the double transcendence of the community, in this way once again bringing out an important element: the faith community does not create itself. It is not an assembly of men who have some ideas in common and who decide to work for the spread of such ideas. Then everything would be based on one's own decision and, in the final analysis, on the principle that the majority rules, which ultimately would be based on human opinion. A Church built in this way cannot be for me the guarantor of eternal life or require me to make decisions that cause me to suffer and are contrary to my desires. No, the Church is not self-made; she was created by God, and she is continuously formed by him. This finds expression in the sacraments, above all in that of baptism: I do not come into the Church through a bureaucratic act but through a sacrament. And this is to say that I am

welcomed into a community that did not originate in itself
and is projected beyond itself.

The ministry that aims to form the spiritual experience
of the faithful must proceed from these fundamental giv-
ens. It needs to abandon the idea of a self-made Church
and to make it clear that the Church becomes a community through the communion of the Body of Christ. She
must bring people to an encounter with Jesus Christ and
into his presence in the sacrament.

*When you were prefect of the Congregation for the Doctrine of
the Faith, commenting on the Joint Declaration of the Catholic
Church and the Lutheran World Federation on the Doctrine of
Justification of 31 October 1999, you pointed out a difference
of mentality in relation to Luther and the question of salvation
and blessedness as he had posed it. Luther's religious experience
was dominated by terror before the wrath of God, a feeling quite
alien to modern men, who instead sense the absence of God (see
your article in* Communio, *German edition [2000]: 430). For
them, the problem is not so much how to obtain eternal life, but
rather how to ensure, in the precarious conditions of our world,
a certain balance of fully human life. Can the teaching of Saint
Paul on justification by faith, in this new context, reach the
"religious" experience or at least the "elementary" experience of
our contemporaries?*

First of all, I want to emphasize once again what I wrote
in *Communio* (2000) on the issue of justification. Today,
compared to the time of Luther and to the classical perspective of the Christian faith, things are in a certain sense
inverted, or rather, man no longer believes he needs justification before God, but rather he is of the opinion that
it is God who must justify himself because of all the horrible things in the world and the misery of mankind, all of

which ultimately depends on him. In this regard, I find it significant that a Catholic theologian could profess even in a direct and formal way this inverted position: that Christ did not suffer for the sins of men, but rather, as it were, to "cancel out the faults of God". Even if most Christians today would not share such a drastic reversal of our faith, we could say that all of this reveals an underlying trend of our times. When Johann Baptist Metz argues that theology today must be "sensitive to theodicy" (German: *theodizee-empfindlich*), this highlights the same problem in a positive way. Even prescinding from such a radical contestation of the Church's understanding of the relationship between God and man, mankind today, in a very general way, has the sense that God cannot allow the majority of humanity to be damned. In this sense, the concern for the personal salvation of souls typical of past times has for the most part disappeared.

However, in my opinion, there continues to exist, in another way, the perception that we are in need of grace and forgiveness. For me, a "sign of the times" is the fact that the notion that God's mercy should be more and more central and dominant—starting with Sister Faustina,[1] whose visions in various ways deeply reflect the image of God held by people today and their desire for divine goodness. Pope John Paul II was deeply imbued with this impulse, even if it did not always emerge explicitly. But it is certainly not by chance that his last book, published just before his death, speaks of God's mercy. Starting from the experiences that, from the earliest years of life, exposed him to all of man's cruelty, he affirms that mercy is the

---

[1] Sister Faustina Kowalska, born in Głogowiec, Poland, in 1905, received mystical graces that prompted her to become the apostle of Divine Mercy. She died in Kraków in 1938. Saint John Paul II, who proclaimed her a saint in the year 2000, was very devoted to her. (Editor's note.)

only true and ultimate effective reaction against the power of evil. Only where there is mercy does cruelty end, do evil and violence end. Pope Francis is totally in agreement with this line. His pastoral practice is expressed in the very fact that he continually speaks to us of God's mercy. It is mercy that moves us toward God, while justice only frightens us before him.

In my view, this makes it clear that, under a veneer of self-assuredness and self-righteousness, mankind today hides a deep awareness of its wounds and unworthiness before God. Mankind is waiting for mercy.

It is certainly no coincidence that the parable of the Good Samaritan is particularly attractive to contemporary man. And not just because that parable strongly empha-sizes the social dimension of Christian existence, nor only because in it the Samaritan, the non-religious man, in comparison with the representatives of religion, seems, so to speak, to be one who acts in true conformity with God, while the official representatives of religion seem, as it were, immune to God. This clearly pleases modern man. It seems just as important to me, however, that men deep in their hearts expect that the Samaritan will come to their aid; that he will bend down to them, anoint their wounds, care for them, and carry them to safety. In the final analysis, they know that they need God's mercy and his tenderness. In the hardness of a technological world where feelings no longer count for anything, nevertheless, there is a growing expectation of a saving love that is freely given. It seems to me that in the theme of divine mercy the meaning of justification by faith is expressed in a new way. Starting from the mercy of God, for which everyone is looking, it is possible even today to interpret anew the fundamental nucleus of the doctrine of justification and have it appear again in all its relevance.

When Anselm says that Christ had to die on the Cross in order to remedy the infinite offense that had been committed against God, and in this way to restore the shattered order, he uses a language that is difficult for modern man to accept (cf. Gaudium et spes, no. 4). Expressing oneself in this way, one risks projecting onto God an image of a God of wrath, relentless toward the sin of man, with feelings of violence and aggression comparable to what we can experience ourselves. How is it possible to speak of God's justice without potentially undermining the certainty, firmly established among the faithful, that the Christian God is a God "rich in mercy" (Eph 2:4)?

The conceptual categories of Saint Anselm have now become for us incomprehensible. It is our task to try to understand anew the truth that lies behind this mode of expression. For my part, I offer three points of view on this perspective:

1. The contrast between the Father who insists in an absolute way on justice and the Son who obeys the Father and, in obeying, accepts the cruel demands of justice is not only incomprehensible today, but, from the standpoint of Trinitarian theology, is in itself all wrong. The Father and the Son are one, and therefore their will is *ab intrinseco* one. When in the Garden of Olives, the Son struggles with the will of the Father, it is a matter, not of accepting for himself some cruel disposition of God, but rather of drawing his humanity into the will of God itself. We will have to come back again, later, to the relationship of the two wills of the Father and of the Son.

2. So why the Cross and the atonement? Somehow today, in the contortions of modern thought mentioned above, the answer to these questions can be formulated in a new way. Let's place ourselves before the obscene amount of evil, violence, falsehood, hatred, cruelty, and

arrogance that infect and destroy the whole world. This mass of evil cannot simply be declared nonexistent, not even by God. It must be cleansed, reworked, and overcome. Ancient Israel was convinced that daily sacrifice for sins and above all the great liturgy of the Day of Atonement (Yom Kippur) were necessary as a counterweight to the mass of evil in the world and that only through such rebalancing could the world, as it were, remain bearable. Once the sacrifices in the Temple disappeared, one had to wonder what could be set against the higher powers of evil, how a counterweight could be found. The Christians knew that the destroyed Temple was replaced by the resurrected Body of the crucified Lord and that in his radical and immeasurable love was created a counterweight to the immeasurable presence of evil. Indeed, they knew that the offerings presented up until then could only be conceived of as a gesture of longing for a genuine counterweight. They also knew that before the excessive power of evil only an infinite love could suffice, only an infinite atonement. They knew that the crucified and risen Christ is a power that can counter the power of evil and save the world.

And on this basis, they could even understand the meaning of their own suffering as integrated into the suffering love of Christ and as part of the redemptive power of such love. Above I quoted the theologian for whom God had to suffer for his sins in regard to the world. Now, due to this reversal of perspective, the following truths emerge: God simply cannot leave "as is" the mass of evil that comes from the freedom that he himself has granted. He alone, by coming to share in the world's suffering, can redeem the world.

3. Based on these premises, the relationship between the Father and the Son becomes more comprehensible. I

would use a passage from a book by Henri de Lubac on Origen which I find very clear on the subject:

> The Savior descended to earth out of pity for the human race. He was subject to our passions before suffering the Cross, before he had even deigned to assume our flesh: for if he had not first been subject to them, he would not have come to participate in our human life.
>
> What is this passion that he first suffered for us? It is the passion of love.
>
> But the Father himself, God of the universe, he who is full of forbearance, mercy, and pity, does he not suffer in some way? Or are you unaware that, when he is occupied with human things, he suffers a human passion? "For the Lord your God has taken your ways upon himself just as one carries his child" [*Homilies on Ezekiel* 6, 6]. God thus takes on our ways, just as the Son of God takes on our passions. The Father himself is not impassible! If one prays to him, he has pity and compassion. He suffers a passion of love.[2]

In some parts of Germany there was a very moving devotion that contemplated the *Not Gottes* ("poverty of God"). For my part, that leads me to see an impressive image of the suffering Father, who, as Father, inwardly shares the sufferings of the Son. And the image of the "throne of grace" is also part of this devotion: the Father supports the Cross and the Crucified One, bends lovingly down to him, and the two are, as it were, one on the Cross. So in a grand and pure way, one perceives there what God's mercy means, what God's participation in human suffering means. It is a matter, not of a cruel justice, nor of the Father's fanaticism, but rather of the truth and the reality

---

[2] Henri de Lubac, *History and Spirit: The Understanding of Scripture according to Origen*, trans. Anne Englund Nash (San Francisco: Ignatius Press, 2007), 275.

of creation: the true intimate overcoming of evil that ultimately can be realized only in the suffering of love.

In the Spiritual Exercises, *Ignatius of Loyola does not use
the Old Testament images of vengeance, in contrast to Paul (cf.
2 Thess 1:5–9); nevertheless he invites us to contemplate how
men, until the Incarnation, "descended into hell" (cf.* Spiritual
Exercises, *no. 102; Heinrich Denzinger,* Enchiridion sym-
bolorum, *ed. Peter Hünermann [San Francisco: Ignatius Press,
2012], no. 464) and to consider the example of the "countless
others who ended up there for far fewer sins than I have committed" (*Spiritual Exercises, *no. 52). It is in this spirit that Saint
Francis Xavier lived his pastoral work, convinced he had to try to
save as many "infidels" as possible from the terrible fate of eternal
damnation. The teaching, formalized in the Council of Trent, in
the passage regarding the judgment of good and evil, later radical-
ized by the Jansenists, was taken up in a much more restrained
way in the* Catechism of the Catholic Church *(cf. nos. 633,
1037). Can it be said on this point that, in recent decades, there
has been a kind of "development of dogma" that the* Catechism
absolutely must take into account?

There is no doubt that on this point we are faced with
a profound evolution of dogma. While the fathers and
theologians of the Middle Ages could still have been of
the opinion that, essentially, the whole human race had
become Catholic and that by that time paganism existed
only on the margins, the discovery of the New World at
the beginning of the modern era radically changed perspectives. In the second half of the last century, it was
fully affirmed: the realization that God cannot abandon
all the unbaptized to damnation and that mere natural
happiness cannot represent a real answer to the question
of human existence. If it is true that the great missionaries

of the sixteenth century were still convinced that those who are not baptized are forever lost—and this explains their missionary commitment—in the Catholic Church after the Second Vatican Council, that conviction was definitively abandoned.

From this came a profound crisis that was twofold. On the one hand, this seems to remove all motivation for a future missionary commitment. Why should one try to convince people to accept the Christian faith when they can save themselves without it? But among Christians, too, an issue emerged: the obligatory nature of the faith and its way of life began to seem uncertain and problematic. If people can save themselves in other ways, it is not clear, in the final analysis, why Christians should be bound by the requirements of Christian faith and morals. If faith and salvation are no longer interdependent, faith has no motive.

Lately several attempts have been formulated with the purpose of reconciling the universal necessity of the Christian faith with the possibility of salvation without it. Here I will mention two: first, Karl Rahner's well-known thesis of anonymous Christians. He maintains that the basic and essential act at the root of Christian existence, which is decisive for salvation, in the transcendental structure of our consciousness, consists in the opening to the Other, to unity with God. In this vision, the Christian faith would raise to consciousness what is structural in man as such. Thus, when a man accepts himself in his essential being, he fulfills the essence of being a Christian without knowing what it is in a conceptual way. The Christian, therefore, coincides with the human, and, in this sense, every man who accepts himself is a Christian even if he does not know it. It is true that this theory is fascinating, but it reduces Christianity itself to a purely conscious presentation of what man is in

himself and therefore overlooks the drama of change and
renewal that is central to Christianity.

Even less acceptable is the solution proposed by the plu-
ralistic theories of religion, according to which all religions,
each in its own way, would be means to salvation and, in
this sense, in their effects must be considered equivalent.
The kind of critique of religion used in the Old Testament
is, in the New Testament and in the early Church, essentially more realistic, more concrete, and truer in its examination of the various religions. Such a simplistic reception
is not proportionate to the magnitude of the issue.

Let us recall, lastly and above all, Henri de Lubac and
with him several other theologians who labored over the
concept of vicarious substitution. For them the "pro-
existence" ("*being-for*") of Christ would be an expression
of the fundamental figure of Christian life and of the
Church as such. It is true that this does not completely
resolve the problem, but it seems to me that in reality this
essential insight touches the life of every single Christian.
Christ, insofar as he is unique, was and is for *all* people,
and Christians, whom Saint Paul magnificently describes
as his Body in the world, participate in this *being-for*.
Christians, so to speak, do not exist for themselves, but,
along with Christ, they exist for others. That does not
mean some kind of special ticket to eternal beatitude,
but, rather, it is a vocation to build up the whole Body.
What the human person needs in the order of salvation is
an interior openness to God, an interior expectation for
and adherence to him. And this in turn means that we
together, with the Lord whom we have encountered, go
forth to others and seek to render visible the coming of
God in Christ.

It is possible to explain this *being-for* in a more abstract
way, also. It is important to mankind that there be truth in

it, that it be believed and practiced. That one should suffer for it. That one should love it. These realities penetrate with their light into the world as such and support it. I think that in this present situation what the Lord said to Abraham becomes for us ever more clear and understandable, that is, that ten righteous men would have sufficed to save a city, but that it would self-destruct if that small number were not reached. It is clear that we need further reflection on the matter as a whole.

In the eyes of many secular humanists, marked by the atheism of the nineteenth and twentieth centuries, as you have noted, it is God—if he exists—not man who should be held accountable for injustice, for the suffering of the innocent, for the cynicism of power we are witnessing, powerless, in the world and in world history (cf. Spe salvi, no. 42). . . . In your book Jesus of Nazareth, *you echo what for them—and for us—is a scandal: "That which is wrong, the reality of evil, cannot simply be ignored; it cannot just be left to stand. It must be dealt with; it must be overcome. Only this counts as true mercy."*[3] *Is the sacrament of confession one of the places where the evil done can be "remedied"? If so, how?*

I have already tried to expose as a whole the main points related to this issue in my answer to your third question. The counterweight to the dominion of evil can consist in the first place only in the divine-human love of Jesus Christ that is always greater than any possible power of evil. But it is necessary that we include ourselves within this answer that God gives us through Jesus Christ. Even if the individual is responsible for a fragment of evil and, therefore, is an accomplice of its power, together with

---

[3] *Jesus of Nazareth: Holy Week . . .*, trans. Philip J. Whitmore (San Francisco: Ignatius Press, 2011), 133, quoting 2 Tim 2:13.

Christ he can nevertheless "complete what is lacking in Christ's afflictions" (Col 1:24).

The sacrament of penance certainly has an important role in this field. It means that we always allow ourselves to be molded and transformed by Christ and that we pass continuously from the side of him who destroys to the side of him who saves.

THE CATHOLIC PRIESTHOOD

Preliminary Methodological Reflection

Vatican II gave us a beautiful document on the Catholic priesthood but did not address the fundamental question that the sixteenth-century Reformation poses to the Catholic priesthood. This question is a wound that silently continues to make itself felt and, in my opinion, must finally be discussed thoroughly and openly. This task is as important as it is difficult because it involves the whole problem of exegesis, the hermeneutic of which is determined by Luther's. The German Reformer starts from the fact that the New Testament ministers are of a different nature compared to the priesthood of the Old Covenant. In the Old Covenant, the central task of the "priest" was to offer sacrifice and thereby to obtain justice in the manner prescribed by the Torah or else to restore the just order in the relation between God and man by means of an action prescribed by God himself. On the contrary, Saint Paul teaches us that no true justification of man can come about in this way, as the critique of worship by the Old Testament prophets, too, had already pointed out clearly. According to Luther, on the other hand, the saving gift of Jesus consists in our being justified *sola fide*—by

"The Catholic Priesthood" was completed in 2018 and published in Robert Cardinal Sarah with Joseph Ratzinger/Benedict XVI, *From the Depths of Our Hearts: Priesthood, Celibacy, and the Crisis of the Catholic Church*, trans. Michael J. Miller (San Francisco: Ignatius Press, 2020), 23–60. The text was subsequently revised and expanded; the new version is published here for the first time.

faith alone and by nothing else. The fundamental act of faith consists in the firm conviction that I am justified. The certainty of faith refers essentially to myself: it is certainty about my justification.[4] Therefore, besides baptism and the Last Supper, no sacrament is necessary, however important the sacrament of penance had been for Luther. But, for him, the essence of the latter was not so much to forgive sins as to instill in me the certainty that they are forgiven. And the pastor's task is essentially to reassure each individual again and again of his own justification. Therefore, the New Testament ministry cannot have a priestly character; unlike the Old Testament priesthood, it has nothing to do with offering a sacrifice; it is structured in an entirely different way. It can consist solely in the proclamation of the faith to the people so as to lead them to faith and in faith.

In contrast to the *priests* of the Old Covenant, the ministers of the New Covenant are "pastors". This radical difference between *sacerdos*, a ministry in service to the Law, and pastoral service can be seen in all its incisiveness when we consider just how far the Law-prescribed attempt to obtain one's own justification through a work (sacrifice) would lead man fundamentally astray. Man believes that in this way he fulfills God's will, which thus far seemed to require sacrifice of him, but in reality, in the Law, speaks *ex contrario* as man's own enemy. In reality, man is said to be justified only by faith. The relation between the two Testaments is described as a dialectic of Law and Gospel, a dialectic attenuated, however, by the fact that in the Old Testament itself, besides the Law, there is the *promissio* (promise) that refers to the future Gospel.

---

[4] Cf. Paul Hacker, *Das Ich im Glauben bei Martin Luther* (Graz: Verlag Styria, 1966).

For Luther, the serious error of Catholic tradition is that, over the course of the first centuries, it once again transformed the New Testament pastoral ministry into *sacerdotium* [Latin: priesthood], so that the German word *Priester*, which is a Germanicization of the word *presbyter* [Greek: elder], contrary to its original New Testament meaning, today in fact means *sacerdos* [priest]. In his view, the Catholic Church had radically falsified the message of the New Testament by abolishing the *sola fide* and putting justification by the Law back in its place. For this reason, Luther considered the Catholic Mass to be as mistaken as the Old Testament sacrifice, and he exhorted his followers to combat it, even with acts of violence.

It is quite clear, therefore, that "Last Supper" and "Mass" are two completely different forms of worship, which by their nature exclude each other. Anyone who preaches intercommunion today ought to remember this.

Luther's entire construct is founded on his concept of the reciprocal relation between the two Testaments, based on the contrast between Law and Gospel, between justification by works and by faith. A Catholic naturally notices that this concept cannot be right; therefore he perceives the Holy Mass, not as an illegitimate relapse into the sacrificial worship of the Old Covenant, but rather as our inclusion in the Body of Christ and therefore in his self-gift to the Father, an act that makes us all become one with him. The conciliar decree on the priesthood, as well as the Vatican II constitution on the liturgy, are supported by this calm certainty, even though, in the concrete implementation of the liturgical reform, Luther's theses silently played a certain role, so that in some circles it could be maintained that the Council of Trent's Decree on the Sacrifice of the Mass had been tacitly abrogated. The harshness of the opposition to the admissibility of the old liturgy was certainly based in part also on the fact that it was viewed as perpetuating a no longer acceptable concept of sacrifice and expiation.

Historical-critical exegesis in turn demonstrated that the New Testament ministries initially did not have a priestly character, but were instead pastoral services. The fusion with the *sacerdotium* of the Old Covenant, however, was then accomplished in a surprisingly rapid way and was not criticized by anyone. This was possible on the basis of a different concept of the relation between Old and New Testament. The early Church never thought of this relation as a contrast between justification by works and justification by faith alone. In the early Church, Luther's theology finds a counterpart only in Marcion, whose theory, however, was immediately ruled out in the early Church because it was considered heretical. The idea of the Law, the Torah, as God's action *ex contrario* is totally foreign to the early Church and directly opposed to its fundamental relation with the Old Testament. For this reason, the *sola fide*, as understood by Luther, was never taught in the early Church. Instead, the relation between the Testaments was thought of as a passage from a material understanding to a Pneumatological understanding (see 2 Cor 3).

This has two implications for our understanding of the Eucharist.

1. The end of the "Old Testament worship" was imposed above all by the destruction of the Temple of Jerusalem. In this sense, it is mankind's fault [*Schuld, colpa*], that is to say, it is due to the destruction of the Temple, for which Jews and pagans (Romans) were in equal measure responsible. This human guilt [*Schuld, colpa*] which led to the definitive destruction is transformed by God into a new path for humanity: "Destroy this temple, and in three days I will raise it up" (Jn 2:19). The demolition of the Temple made of stone signifies at the same time the crucifixion of

Jesus. Instead of a stone temple, there is Jesus Christ, risen on the third day in his Body. The old Temple is destroyed forever, and with it the Old Covenant order of sacrifices is abolished also. Unlike the preceding destructions of the Temple, this one is now definitive. Even today, now that the state of Israel has supreme jurisdiction over the Temple Mount, no one is thinking of rebuilding it. The final attempt that occurred with Bar Kochba (in A.D. 135) corresponds to the definitive and irrevocable loss of the stone temple. Instead of the worship with animal sacrifices, there is Jesus Crucified. His offering of love to the Father is the true worship, as the Letter to the Hebrews forcefully shows. At the same time, it is the definitive worship that can be replaced by nothing superior, because there is nothing superior to the love of the Son of God made man, which summarizes in itself and transforms all the sacrifices of the world.

2. At the Last Supper, Jesus conferred on his sacrificial offering to the Father the perennial form in which from then on the Church in every place and time can join herself to his offering. In the words of the Last Supper, he joined the Sinai tradition to the prophetic tradition and thereby truly instituted the "worship" of the New Covenant, in which worship and lovingly listening to the Word of God—which becomes service to one's neighbor, love of neighbor—are one and the same thing. The redemption of mankind consists, not in a kind of Marcionite *sola fide*, but rather in an ever more profound union with the love of Jesus Christ. Thus man still remains challenged and is still on a journey and, at the same time, is still already accepted by means of the ever-increasing love of Jesus Christ.

Obviously the spirit of modernity, and the historical-critical method derived from it, finds itself more at ease with Luther's solution than with the Catholic one, because a "Pneumatological" exegesis, which understands the Old Testament as a way toward Jesus Christ, is almost inaccessible to it. Nevertheless, it is clear that Jesus thought, not along the lines of a radical *sola fide*, but rather along the lines of a fulfillment of the Law and the Prophets in his own journey and in his being. The task of the new generation is to create the conditions—methodological as well—for a renewed understanding of what was just said.

The Formation of the New Testament Priesthood in Christological-Pneumatological Exegesis

The movement that had formed around Jesus of Nazareth—at least during the pre-Paschal period—was a movement of laymen. In this respect, it resembled the movement of the Pharisees, and this is why the first conflicts described in the Gospels refer essentially to the Pharisaical movement. Only at the time of the last *Pesach* [Passover] of Jesus in Jerusalem did the priestly aristocracy of the Temple—the Sadducees—notice Jesus and his movement, which led to the trial, the condemnation, and the execution of Jesus. Consequently, the ministries of the community that started to form around Jesus could not be part of the framework of the Old Testament priesthood. The [Temple] priesthood was hereditary: a man who was not descended from a family of priests could not become a priest.

Now let us take a look at the ministries that began to form in the pre-Paschal community.

Apostolos

The essential ministry instituted by Jesus is that of apostle. The word "apostle", in the political-institutional language of Hellenism, means someone to whom a message is entrusted.[5] The important thing is that the one so charged, within the scope of the mandate entrusted to him, is like the principal himself. Rabbinical language is familiar with the word in an analogous sense. Mark refers to the institution of the apostles with words that are both concise and significant: "He appointed twelve (whom also he named apostles) to be with him, and to be sent out to preach and have authority to cast out demons" (Mk 3:14–15 [the parenthetical phrase is found in some ancient manuscripts]). Next Mark repeats once again the words of the institution: "He appointed twelve" and then lists the names of the twelve who were called (Mk 3:16–19). In Matthew 28:16, the risen Jesus broadens the mandate, extending the mission to all nations.

With regard to the fundamental words of institution in Mark 3, however, it must be pointed out that initially the word "apostle" was not used, but rather it says: "He appointed twelve." Only after that does the statement follow; "whom he named apostles". Accordingly, Matthew 28:16ff. does not speak about apostles but about eleven disciples. As everyone knows, the eleven considered the number twelve of this college so important that they restored it by co-optation.

In this sense, the expressions "the twelve" and "the apostles" are practically equivalent, and very soon they were firmly joined in the formula "twelve apostles", so that only someone who belonged to the circle of the twelve could also be called an apostle. This posed a problem for Saint Paul, who nevertheless knew that he belonged to the circle of the twelve apostles and was of the same rank as they.

---

[5] *Theologisches Wörterbuch zum Neuen Testament*, 11 vols., new ed. (Darmstadt: WBG Academic, 2019), 1:397–448.

As a whole it is permissible to suppose that the close connection between "twelve" and "apostles" developed only gradually, albeit very early on. Therefore, if we consider the twelve as an arrangement willed by Jesus himself, the new element that Jesus intended to bring emerges very clearly. Indeed, the twelve refer to the twelve sons of Jacob, from whom the people of Israel developed. Opposite them stand the additional seventy belonging to the house of Jacob, who indicate the number of the nations on earth. The original idea of Jesus, consequently, was to conceive of himself, through the calling of the "twelve", as fountainhead of the new Israel—a claim that went beyond all the common expectations concerning salvation. In this sense, it goes well beyond the idea of lay collaborators, even though there is no direct mention of priesthood.

Episkopos

In Greek, in everyday language, the word *episkopos* indicates functions associated with tasks of a technical and financial nature. However, it also has a religious sense, inasmuch as the ones who are called *episkopos* are most often the gods, that is to say, protectors or patrons. "The Septuagint uses the word *episkopos* in the two senses already in use in the pagan Greek world: on the one hand, as a name of God and, on the other hand, in the profane and generic sense of 'overseer'."[6]

Presbyteros

While among the Christians of Gentile origin, the term *episkopos* is most often used to refer to ministers, the word *presbyteros* is characteristic of the Judeo-Christian milieu. In

[6] Ibid., 2:610, lines 6–19.

Jerusalem, the Jewish tradition of the "elders", considered as a sort of constitutional body, obviously developed rapidly into an initial form of Christian ministry. From then on, the Church composed of Jews and Gentiles showed the development of the threefold form of ministry composed of bishops, priests, and deacons. We find it already clearly developed in the late first century in the writings of Ignatius of Antioch. To this day, it has expressed appropriately the ministerial structure of the Church of Jesus Christ both terminologically and ontologically.

From the preceding remarks it is clear that the lay character of Jesus' first movement and the character of the first ministries, understood not in a cultic-priestly sense, are not necessarily based at all on an anti-cultic and anti-Jewish choice but, rather, are a consequence of the particular situation of the Old Testament priesthood, in which the priesthood is reserved exclusively to the tribe of Aaron-Levi. In the two other "lay movements" at the time of Jesus, the relation with the priesthood is thought of differently: the Pharisees seem to have lived basically in harmony with the Temple hierarchy, except for the dispute about the resurrection of the body. Among the Essenes, the movement in Qumran, the situation is more complex. In any case, one part of the Qumran movement was marked by its opposition to the Herodian Temple and to the priesthood that corresponded to it, not in order to deny the priesthood, but rather to reconstitute it in its pure, correct form. Similarly, in Jesus' movement, it is not at all a question of "desacralization", "delegalization", or a rejection of priesthood and hierarchy. On the contrary, the prophets' critique of worship is certainly taken up again, but it is unified in a surprising way with the priestly and cultic tradition in a synthesis that we must attempt to understand. In my book *The Spirit of the Liturgy*, I explained the different critiques of the prophets concerning worship. They were taken up again by Stephen, and Saint Paul links them with the new cultic tradition of the Last Supper of Jesus. Jesus himself had repeated and approved the prophets' critique of worship, especially on the subject of the dispute over the correct interpretation of the *Shabbat* (cf. Mt 12:7–8).

Let us examine first Jesus' relation with the Temple as the expression of God's special presence in the midst of his chosen people and as the place of worship regulated by Moses. The episode of the twelve-year-old Jesus in the Temple shows that his family was observant and that he himself participated in the devotion of his own family. The words that he said to his mother—"Did you not know that I must be in my Father's house?" (Lk 2:49)—express the conviction that the Temple represents in a special way the place where God dwells and, therefore, the right place for the Son to reside in. Similarly, during the short period of his public life, Jesus participated in Israel's pilgrimages to the Temple, and, after his Resurrection, it is well known that his community assembled regularly in the Temple for teaching and prayers.

And yet, through the cleansing of the Temple, Jesus introduced a fundamentally new emphasis concerning the Temple (Mk 11:15ff.; Jn 2:13–22). The interpretation whereby the sole intention of this gesture of Jesus was to combat abuses and thus to confirm the function of the Temple is inadequate. In John, we find words that interpret Jesus' action as a prefiguration of the destruction of this building made of stone, in place of which his own Body would appear as the new Temple. In the Synoptic Gospels, this interpretation of Jesus' words appears on the lips of false witnesses at his trial (Mk 14:58). The witnesses' version was distorted, and therefore it could not be used to help determine the trial's outcome. But the fact remains that Jesus did make similar statements, even though the exact words could not be determined with sufficient certainty during the trial. The nascent Church was therefore correct to assume that the Johannine version was authentically from Jesus. This means that Jesus considers the destruction of the Temple to be the consequence of the erroneous attitude of the ruling priestly hierarchy. Nevertheless, as at every crucial moment in salvation history, God utilizes here the erroneous behavior of men as a *modus* [means] of manifesting his greater love. At this level, obviously, Jesus ultimately considers the destruction of the Temple that existed then as a stage in the divine healing and interprets it as the formation and organization of a new and definitive worship. In this sense, the cleansing of the Temple is the announcement of a new form of divine adoration, and consequently it concerns the nature of worship and of the priesthood in general.

Of course the Last Supper, with the offering of the Body and Blood of Jesus Christ, is decisive for an understanding of what Jesus intended and what he did not intend on the subject of worship. This is not the place to enter into the controversy that developed later over the correct interpretation of this event and of Jesus' words. The important thing is that Jesus, on the one hand, adopts the tradition of Sinai and thus presents himself as the new Moses; on the other hand, though, he adopts the hope for the New Covenant that was formulated in a particular way by Jeremiah. He thus announces a development beyond the Sinai tradition, at the center of which he himself stands as the one sacrificing and at the same time as the victim. It is indeed necessary to consider that this Jesus who stands in the midst of his disciples is the same one who gives himself to them in his flesh and in his blood, thus anticipating the Cross and the Resurrection. Without the Resurrection, all this would have no meaning. The crucifixion of Jesus is not in itself a cultic act. The Roman soldiers who execute him are not priests. They carry out an execution, but have not even the slightest thought of performing an act of worship. The fact that Jesus gives himself forever as food in the Upper Room during the Last Supper signifies the anticipation of his death and Resurrection and the transformation of an act of human cruelty into an act of love and self-giving. Thus Jesus himself accomplishes the fundamental renewal of worship that will forever remain valid and obligatory. He transforms the sin of men into an act of forgiveness and love into which his future disciples can enter by participating in what Jesus instituted. In this way we understand also what Saint Augustine calls the transition, in the Church, from the Last Supper to the morning sacrifice. The Last Supper is the gift that God grants us in the love of Jesus Christ who forgives and allows humanity in turn to receive this gesture of love from God and to return it to God.

In all this, nothing is said directly about the priesthood. However, it is clearly evident that the former order of Aaron is outmoded and that Jesus himself appears as the High Priest. It is important, furthermore, that in this way the critique of worship by the prophets and the cultic tradition that goes back to Moses merge: love and sacrifice. In my book on Jesus,[7] I explained how this new foundation of worship and, with it, of the priesthood is already entirely completed in the writings of Saint Paul. It is a fundamental unity [of love and sacrifice], based on the mediation established by the death and Resurrection of Jesus. It was clearly admitted even by the adversaries of Paul's proclamation.

[7] Joseph Ratzinger/Benedict XVI, *Jesus of Nazareth*, vol. 2, *From the Entrance into Jerusalem to the Resurrection*, trans. Philip J. Whitmore (San Francisco: Ignatius Press, 2011), 38–41.

The destruction of the Temple walls, caused by man, is accepted in a positive way by God. There are no more walls; instead, the Risen Christ has become for mankind the space in which to adore God. In this way, the collapse of the Herodian Temple also signifies that now nothing divisive comes between the linguistic and existential space of the Mosaic legislation, on the one hand, and the space of the movement gathered around Jesus, on the other hand. The Christian ministries (*episkopos, presbyteros, diakonos*) and those that were regulated by the Mosaic Law (high priests, priests, Levites) from now on stand openly side by side and can also be identified with one another now with a new clarity. Indeed, the terminological equivalence comes about rather quickly (*episkopos* = high priest, *presbyteros* = priest, *diakonos* = Levite). We find it quite clearly in the catecheses on baptism by Saint Ambrose, which certainly refer to older models and documents. What is happening here is no less than the christological interpretation of the Old Testament, which can also be called a Pneumatological interpretation. This is how the Old Testament was able to become and to remain the Bible of the Christians. Although, on the one hand, this christological-Pneumatological interpretation could also be called "allegorical" from a historical-literary perspective, on the other hand, it plainly illustrates the profound novelty and the clear motivation of the new Christian interpretation of the Old Testament. Here allegory is not a literary expedient so as to make the text applicable to new purposes but, rather, the expression of a historical transition that corresponds to the internal logic of the text.

The Cross of Jesus Christ is the act of radical love in which reconciliation really is accomplished between God and the world marred by sin. This is the reason why this event, which in itself is by no means of a cultic type, represents instead the supreme adoration of God. In the Cross, the "katabatic" line of descent from God and the "anabatic" line of humanity's offering to God become a single act, made possible by the new temple of Christ's Body in the Resurrection. In the celebration of the Eucharist, the Church and even humanity are drawn again and again into this process and involved in it. In the Cross of Christ, the critique of worship by the prophets definitively reaches its goal. At the same time, though, the new worship is instituted. The love of Christ, which is always present in the Eucharist, is the new act of adoration. Consequently, the priestly ministries of Israel are "annulled" in the service of love, which still signifies concomitantly the adoration of God. This new unity of love and worship, of critique of worship and glorification of God in the service of love, is certainly an unprecedented task that has been entrusted to the Church and that must be renewed in every generation.

Thus, the Pneumatic overcoming of the Old Testament "letter" in the New Covenant continuously requires a passage from the "letter" to the spirit. In the sixteenth century, Luther, who based his teaching on a completely different reading of the Old Testament, could no longer make this passage. For this reason, he interpreted Old Testament worship and the priesthood that was designed for it solely as an expression of the Law, which for him was not part of the path of God's grace but was opposed to it. Consequently, he had to see a radical opposition between the New Testament ministerial offices and the priesthood as such. At the time of Vatican II, this question became absolutely unavoidable for the Catholic Church as well. "Allegory" as a Pneumatic transition from the Old to the New Testament had become incomprehensible. And while the council's Decree on the Ministry and Life of Priests hardly deals with this question, after the council it monopolized our attention with an unprecedented urgency and turned into a crisis of the priesthood in the Church that has lasted to this day.

Two personal observations may illustrate this statement. It has remained engraved on my memory how one of my friends, the great India expert Paul Hacker, confronted this question with his customary impetuous passion in his conversion from being a staunch Lutheran to a Catholic. He considered "priests" to be an institution outmoded once and for all in the New Testament. With passionate indignation, he was opposed above all to the fact that in the German word *Priester*, which comes from the Greek term *presbyteros* [elder], the connotation of *sacerdotium* [Latin: priesthood] continued to resonate in spite of everything— and this is true. I no longer know how he finally managed to resolve this question.

I myself, during a conference on priesthood in the Church that was held immediately after the council, thought that I had to present the priest of the New Testament as the one who meditates on the Word, and not as a "craftsman of worship". It is true that meditation on the Word of God is an important and fundamental task of the priest of God in the New Covenant. Even so, this Word was made flesh. To meditate on it always means also to be nourished by the flesh that is given to us as bread from heaven in the Most Holy Eucharist. To meditate on the Word in the Church of the New Covenant is also a continually renewed abandonment of self to the flesh of Jesus Christ. This self-abandonment is at the same time an acceptance of our own transformation by means of the Cross.

I will return to this subject farther on. For the moment, let us examine several stages in the concrete development of the history of the Church.

We can observe a first step in the institution of a new ministry. The Acts of the Apostles mention the excessive workload of the apostles, who, in addition to their task of preaching and of leading the Church's prayer, at the same time had to take upon themselves full responsibility for the care of the poor. One result of this was that the Hellenistic part of the nascent Church felt neglected. So the apostles decided to devote themselves entirely to prayer and the service of the Word. For charitable works, they created the ministry of the Seven, which was later identified with the diaconate. Moreover, the example of Saint Stephen shows that this ministry, too, required not only purely practical work of a charitable nature, but also the Spirit and faith and, therefore, the ability to serve the Word.

One problem, which has remained crucial to this day, arose from the fact that the new ministries were based, not on familial descent, but on election and vocation. In the case of the priestly hierarchy of Israel, continuity was assured by God himself, because in the final analysis he was the one who gave children to parents. The new ministries, on the contrary, were based, not on membership in a family, but on a vocation given by God and acknowledged by the man [i.e., the recipient]. This is why, in the New Testament community, the problem of vocations arises from the very beginning: "Pray therefore the Lord of the harvest to send out laborers into his harvest" (Mt 9:38). In every generation, it is always the hope and concern of the Church to find some who are called. We know all too well how great a worry and a task this is for the Church, especially today.

There is a further question that is directly connected with this problem. Soon—we do not know exactly when, but in any case very rapidly—the regular and even daily celebration of the Eucharist became essential for the Church. The "supersubstantial" bread is at the same time the "daily" bread of the Church. This, however, had an important consequence, which is precisely what roils the Church today.[8]

In the common awareness of Israel, it was obvious that priests were strictly obliged to observe sexual abstinence during the times when they led worship and were therefore in contact with the divine mystery. The relation between sexual abstinence and divine worship was absolutely clear in the common awareness of Israel. By way of example, I wish to recall the episode in which David, while fleeing Saul, asked the priest Ahimelech to give him some bread: "The priest answered David, 'I have no common bread at hand, but there is holy bread; if only the young men have kept themselves from women.' And David answered the priest, 'Of a truth women have been kept from us as always when I go on an expedition'" (1 Sam 21:4–5). Since the Old Testament priests had to dedicate themselves to worship only during set times, marriage and the priesthood were of course compatible.

But because of the regular or in many cases daily celebration of the Eucharist, the situation for the priests of the Church of Jesus Christ was changed radically. From then on, their entire life was in contact with the divine mystery. This required on their part an exclusive dedication to God that excluded another tie that, like marriage, involves one's whole life. Based on the daily celebration of the Eucharist, and based on the service to God that this

---

[8] About the meaning of the word *epioúsios (supersubstantialis)*, see Eckhard Nordhofen, "What Bread Is This? What Bread This Is!", *Communo: International Catholic Review* 44/1 (2017): 43–71; Gerd Neuhaus, "Möglichkeit und Grenzen einer Gottespräsenz im menschlichen 'Fleisch': Anmerkungen zu Eckhard Nordhofens Relektüre der vierten Vaterunser-Bitte" [Possibility and limits of a divine presence in human 'flesh': Remarks on Eckhard Nordhofen's rereading of the fourth petition of the Our Father], *Internazionale katholische Zeitschrift Communio* 46/1 (2017): 23–32.

entailed, the impossibility of a matrimonial bond followed automatically. One could say that the functional sexual abstinence was transformed automatically into an ontological abstinence. In this way, its motivation and its meaning were changed from within and profoundly.

Nowadays, though, we hear the facile objection that all this was just the result of a contempt for corporeality and sexuality. The critique claiming that priestly celibacy was founded on a Manichaean concept of the world was formulated as early as the fourth century. This critique was immediately and decisively rejected, however, by the Fathers of the Church, and then for a time it disappeared.

A diagnosis of this sort is wrong, if only because, from the beginning in the Church, marriage was considered to be a gift given by God in paradise. However, the married state involved a man in his totality, and serving the Lord likewise required the total gift of a man, so that it did not seem possible to live out the two vocations together. Thus, the ability to renounce marriage so as to be totally at the Lord's disposal became a criterion for priestly ministry.

As for the concrete form of celibacy in the early Church, it should also be emphasized that married men could receive the sacrament of Holy Orders only if they had pledged to observe sexual abstinence, therefore, to live in a so-called "Josephite" marriage, like the marriage of Saint Joseph and the Virgin Mary. This seems to have been quite normal during the first centuries. Clearly there were enough men and women who considered it reasonable and possible to live in this way while together dedicating themselves to the Lord.[9]

---

[9] The reader can find extensive information on the history of celibacy in the first centuries in Stefan Heid, *Celibacy in the Early Church: The Beginnings of a Discipline of Obligatory Continence for Clerics in East and West*, trans. Michael J. Miller (San Francisco: Ignatius Press, 2000; original German edition 1997).

Three Textual Analyses

The preceding reflections clearly showed how profoundly, on the basis of a christological reading of the Old Testament, Jesus of Nazareth is also a priest in the proper sense. However, he cannot bear the title, which is connected with membership in the tribe of Aaron-Levi, since Jesus belonged to the tribe of Judah. A new step in this direction was made by the Letter to the Hebrews. German exegesis had always considered it a stepdaughter [i.e., problematic], because it teaches that Jesus should be understood also and in an absolutely crucial way as high priest, a perspective that could not be reconciled with Luther's hermeneutic. Meanwhile, though, the French Jesuit Albert Cardinal Vanhoye, long-time professor at the Pontifical Biblical Institute in Rome, dedicated his entire life's work to understanding the Letter to the Hebrews, thus giving us the opportunity to appropriate again this truly precious document. But even on the German side, things have started to shift. In this sense, I refer in particular to the excellent commentary on the Letter to the Hebrews written by Knut Backhaus for the *Regensburger Neues Testament*.[10]

The author of the Letter to the Hebrews—who lived completely in the context of the theology of worship described by Saint Stephen and developed in all its depth by Saint Paul—discovers in Genesis 14:17–20 and in Psalm 110 the answer to the question of the priesthood of Jesus contained in these texts. When Abram frees his nephew Lot from captivity, recovering all his goods, the king of Sodom goes out to meet him first, but he pays no attention to him. Then the mysterious figure of Melchizedek,

---

[10] Knut Backhaus, "Der Hebräerbrief", in *Regensburger Neues Testament* (Regensburg: Verlag Friedrich Pustet, 2009).

the king of Salem, appears on the scene: "[He] brought out bread and wine; he was priest of God Most High. And he blessed [Abram] and said, 'Blessed be Abram by God Most High, maker of heaven and earth; and blessed be God Most High, who has delivered your enemies into your hand!' And Abram gave him a tenth of everything" (Gen 14:18–20). Just a few words to depict a powerful figure. Melchizedek, whose name means king of justice, is king of Salem, in other words, of Jerusalem. In this way, on the one hand, he is connected with the tradition of Jerusalem; on the other hand, the local tradition becomes more profound with regard to the authentic center of the discourse: he is king of peace. In addition to that, he is a priest of God Most High. Also mysterious is the reference to bread and wine, offerings that are interpreted as a pre-figuration of the Eucharistic offering. And finally it says about him that he is a priest of God Most High and that he blesses those who are present. With his offering of the tithe, Abram recognizes him as having the prerogatives of a high priest.

Early Judaism and at the same time the Fathers of the Church dedicated themselves lovingly to the interpretation of this figure, who to the Fathers necessarily appeared in several ways as a prefiguration of Jesus Christ.

While at the beginning of salvation history, Melchizedek appears to be defined by the Law and by its ordinances, in Psalm 110 he is depicted as a promise for the future. Psalm 110 is the messianic psalm most often cited in the New Testament. It is distinguished by the absence in it of the fundamental words "king" and "throne", which in contrast occur in the other messianic psalms. Here it says about him that he was generated mysteriously "before the day star" "from the womb of the morning". These are mythical images that, however, would serve later on to prefigure the mystery of the Son. Next come the fundamental words of the promise that repeat the vision of Genesis 14 and become a central aspect of the future salvation: "The LORD has sworn and will not change his mind, 'You are a priest for ever according to the order of Melchizedek'" (Ps 110:4). In this way, the figure that we encounter beside Abram at the beginning of salvation history refers to the future: the savior who will come is above all a priest, and precisely "according to the order of Melchizedek". Based on the stipulation of the covenant on Mount Sinai, in Israel there is a high priest according to the order of Aaron. Psalm 110 instructs us about the fact that in the future there will be another high priest "according to the order of Melchizedek", thus resolving the problem that arose from the limitation of the priesthood to the fleshly descendants of Aaron and Levi. The "order of Melchizedek" discloses a new mode of the high priest's ministry. Jesus is truly high priest, although not according to the order of Aaron. In the preceding paragraph we saw how this priesthood is totally new and different from the Aaronic priesthood, and how it nevertheless fully takes on the significance of *sacerdotium*, in other words, a ministry of sacrifice in the presence of God. This clarified at the same time the priestly character of the ministries that before the discovery of the "order of Melchizedek" could not be configured as *sacerdotium*.

Next I would like to show, through several examples, how the new ministries assumed the priestly character. It is clear that in adopting the concepts of *sacerdos* and *sacerdotium*, there was always a danger of disregarding the radical transformation of the ministry of sacrifice that had taken place in the Cross of Christ. In this sense, the fear from which Luther started out is by no means unfounded, even though the conclusions that led the German Reformer into error do not necessarily follow from it. I would like to interpret now three texts that were decisively helpful to me in my journey to the priesthood. The choice of the texts is connected to my personal story and therefore altogether arbitrary. An essential part of them, following the Spiritual Exercises that Albert Cardinal Vanhoye[11] preached to us in the Vatican in 2008, is the new concept of the priesthood in the Letter to the Hebrews, especially as it is presented on pages 38–39. I hope that a good translation into German of this important book will soon be available.

1. Psalm 16:5–6: the words used for admission to the clerical state before the council

First we have the interpretation of the words of a psalm that were given to me on the day before my admission to the clerical state in May 1948. The passage is Psalm 16:5–6. These words were recited by the bishop, then repeated by the candidate: "*Dominus pars hereditatis meae et calicis mei; tu es qui restitues hereditatem meam mihi*": "The LORD is my chosen portion and my cup; you hold my lot. The lines have fallen for me in pleasant places; yes, I have a goodly heritage" (Ps 16:5–6). Indeed, the psalm expresses, in the Old Testament, exactly what it means later on in the Church: acceptance into the priestly community. This passage refers to the fact that all the tribes of Israel, every single family, was included in the heritage promised by God to Abraham. More concretely, the promise was expressed in the fact that each family obtained as its inheritance a portion of the Promised Land as its property. Possession of a part of the Holy Land gave to each individual the certainty

[11] Albert Cardinal Vanhoye, *Accogliamo Cristo nostro Sommo Sacerdote: Esercizi Spirituali con Benedetto XVI* (Vatican City: LEV, 2008).

of sharing in the promise, and in practice it assured him of a livelihood. Each man had to obtain as much land as he needed in order to live. The story of Naboth (1 Kings 21:1–29), who absolutely refuses to give his vineyard away to King Ahab, even though the latter says that he is willing to reimburse him completely, clearly shows how important this concrete inheritance was for the individual. For Naboth, the vineyard is more than a valuable plot of land: it is his share in God's promise to Israel. Whereas, on the one hand, each Israelite thus had at his disposal a tract of land that assured him of what he needed in order to live, the tribe of Levi had a peculiar feature: it was the only tribe that did not inherit land. The Levite remained without land and was therefore deprived of an immediate subsistence derived from the land. He lived only by God and for God. In practice, this means that he had to live, according to precise norms, on the sacrificial offerings that Israel set aside for God.

This Old Testament prefiguration is fulfilled in the priests of the Church in a new and deeper way: they must live only by God and for him. Saint Paul's writings, above all, clearly spell out what this means concretely. From now on he lives on what people give him, because he gives them the Word of God that is our authentic bread and our true life. Whereas the Levites renounced the possession of land, in the New Testament this privation is transformed, and the renunciation of marriage and family that follows from this radical being-for-God is visible. The Church interpreted the word "clergy" (*clerus* = hereditary allotment) in this sense. To enter the clergy means to renounce a self-centered life and to accept God alone as the support and guarantee of one's own life.

I still have a vivid memory of meditating on this psalm verse on the eve of receiving the tonsure, when I understood what the Lord wanted of me at that moment: he himself wanted to have my life completely at his disposal and, at the same time and in the same way, to entrust himself entirely to me. Thus I could consider the words of this psalm in their entirety as my allotment: "The LORD is my chosen portion and my cup; you hold my lot. The lines have fallen for me in pleasant places; yes, I have a goodly heritage" (Ps 16:5–6).

2. Deuteronomy 10:8 (again in Deut 18:5–8): the words incorporated into Eucharistic Prayer II—the role of the tribe of Levi reinterpreted from a christological and Pneumatological perspective for the priests of the Church

It was exciting news that the liturgical reform after Vatican Council II offered the possibility to choose from among four Eucharistic Prayers. Until then, the Roman liturgy—unlike the Eastern liturgies—had known only one. Till that time, the only valid one was the first, the Roman Canon.

Secondly, let us look now at a Eucharistic Prayer taken from the *Apostolic Tradition* by Saint Hippolytus (died around 235), which therefore goes back to the first half of the third century. Besides the Latin version, the text is attested in various language regions of the early Church, especially in Egypt. The Benedictine monk Bernard Botte provided us, in 1962, with an excellent presentation of the texts and a history of their transmission. The *Traditio* was never an official liturgical text. Hippolytus intended to offer in it some criteria for an orthodox Eucharistic Prayer. For various reasons, the liturgical reform made it an official part of the renewed Roman liturgy. Evidently it intended in this way to make known the fundamental structure of a Eucharistic Prayer, as well as its essential statements. In any case, in the first years of the liturgical reform, the Canon of

Hippolytus was in fact the most-used Eucharistic Prayer of the renewed liturgy.

I was particularly moved by the sentence that illustrates the position of the priest: "Domine, panem vitae et calicem salutis offerimus, gratias agentes quia nos dignos habuisti astare coram te et tibi ministrare." (We offer you, Lord, the Bread of life and the Chalice of salvation, giving thanks that you have held us worthy to be in your presence and minister to you.) This sentence does not mean, as some liturgists would have us believe, that even during the Eucharistic Prayer the priests and the faithful ought to stand and not kneel.[12] We can deduce the correct understanding of this sentence by reflecting that it is taken literally from Deuteronomy 10:8 (again in Deut 18:5–8), where the essential cultic role of the tribe of Levi is described: "At that time the LORD set apart the tribe of Levi to carry the ark of the covenant of the LORD, to stand before the LORD to minister to him and to bless in his name" (Deut 10:8). "For the LORD your God has chosen him out of all your tribes, to stand and minister in the name of the LORD, him and his sons for ever" (Deut 18:5).

These words, which in Deuteronomy serve to define the essence of the priesthood, were later incorporated into the Eucharistic Prayer of the Church of Jesus Christ, thus expressing the continuity and the newness of the priesthood in the New Covenant. What was said formerly

---

[12] While the official German translation of Eucharistic Prayer II says correctly: "vor dir zu stehen und dir zu dienen" (to stand before you and minister to you), the Italian translation simplifies the text, omitting the image of standing in God's presence. Indeed, it says: "Ti rendiamo grazie di averci ammessi alla tua presenza a compiere il servizio sacerdotale" (We give you thanks for having admitted us into your presence to perform the priestly service). [The English translation, as given in the third edition of the Roman Missal (2011), makes a similar simplification, substituting "be in your presence" for the word "stand", as seen above. (Editor's note.)]

about the tribe of Levi and concerned it exclusively is now
applied to the priests and the bishops of the Church.

Following a notion inspired by the Reformation, one
might be prompted to say that this is a relapse from the
newness of the community of Jesus Christ into an outmoded cultic priesthood that should be rejected. Quite
the contrary, it is precisely the step forward of the New
Covenant that takes up the old priesthood into itself and
at the same time transforms it by elevating it to the height
of Jesus Christ. Priesthood is no longer a matter of membership in a family; rather, it is open to humanity on a
vast scale. It is no longer the administration of the sacrifice
in the Temple; rather, it gathers humanity in the love of
Jesus Christ, which embraces the whole world. Worship
and the critique of worship, liturgical sacrifice, and the
service of love for neighbor have now become one. For
this reason, this sentence does not speak about an exterior attitude. Rather, it represents a deeper point of unity
between the Old and the New Testament, and it describes
the very nature of the priesthood, which in turn refers, not
to a determinate class of persons, but in the final analysis to
the fact that we all stand before God.

I tried to interpret this text in a homily given in Saint
Peter's in Rome on Holy Thursday 2008; I cite here an
excerpt from it:

> At the same time Holy Thursday is an occasion for us
> to ask ourselves over and over again: to what did we say
> our "yes"? What does this "being a priest of Jesus Christ"
> mean? The Second Canon of our Missal ... describes
> the essence of the priestly ministry with the words with
> which, in the Book of Deuteronomy (18:5–7), the essence
> of the Old Testament priesthood is described: *astare coram
> te et tibi ministrare* [to stand and minister in the name of
> the Lord]. There are therefore two duties that define the

essence of the priestly ministry: in the first place, "to stand in the Lord's presence". In the *Book of Deuteronomy*, this is read in the context of the preceding [regulation], according to which priests do not receive any portion of land in the Holy Land—they live of God and for God. They did not attend to the usual work necessary to sustain daily life. Their profession was to "stand in the Lord's presence"—to look to him, to be there for him. Hence, ultimately, the word indicated a life in God's presence, and with this also a ministry of representing others. As the others cultivated the land, from which the priest also lived, so he kept the world open to God, he had to live with his gaze on him.

Now if this word is found in the Canon of the Mass immediately after the consecration of the gifts, after the entrance of the Lord in the assembly of prayer, then for us this points to being before the Lord present, that is, it indicates the Eucharist as the center of priestly life. But here too, the meaning is deeper.

During Lent the hymn that introduces the Office of Readings of the Liturgy of the Hours—the Office that monks once recited during the night vigil before God and for humanity—one of the duties of Lent is described with the imperative: *arctius perstemus in custodia*—we must be even more intensely alert. In the tradition of Syrian monasticism, monks were [described] as "those who remained standing". This standing was an expression of vigilance. What was considered here as a duty of the monks, we can rightly see also as an expression of the priestly mission and as a correct interpretation of the word of Deuteronomy: the priest must be on the watch. He must be on his guard in the face of the imminent powers of evil. He must keep the world awake for God. He must be the one who remains standing: upright before the trends of time. Upright in truth. Upright in the commitment for good. Being before the Lord must always also include, at its depths, responsibility for humanity to the Lord, who in his turn takes on the burden of all of us to the Father. And it must be a taking on of him, of Christ, of his word,

his truth, his love. The priest must be upright, fearless and
prepared to sustain even offences for the Lord, as referred
to in the Acts of the Apostles: they were "rejoicing that
they were counted worthy to suffer dishonor for the
name" of Jesus (5:41).

Now let us move on to the second word that the Second Canon repeats from the Old Testament text—"to
stand in your presence and serve you". The priest must be
an upright person, vigilant, a person who remains standing. Service is then added to all this. In the Old Testament
text this word has an essentially ritualistic meaning: all acts
of worship foreseen by the Law are the priests' duty. But
this action, according to the rite, was classified as service,
as a duty of service, and thus it explains in what spirit
this activity must take place. With the assumption of the
word "serve" in the Canon, the liturgical meaning of this
term was adopted in a certain way—to conform with the
novelty of the Christian cult [= worship]. What the priest
does at that moment, in the Eucharistic celebration, is to
serve, to fulfill a service to God and a service to humanity. The cult that Christ rendered to the Father was the
giving of himself to the end for humanity. Into this cult,
this service, the priest must insert himself. Thus, the word
"serve" contains many dimensions. In the first place, part
of it is certainly the correct celebration of the liturgy and
of the sacraments in general, accomplished through interior participation. We must learn to understand increasingly the Sacred Liturgy in all its essence, to develop a
living familiarity with it, so that it becomes the soul of our
daily life. It is then that we celebrate in the correct way; it
is then that the *ars celebrandi*, the art of celebrating, emerges
by itself. In this art there must be nothing artificial. If the
liturgy is the central duty of the priest, this also means
that prayer must be a primary reality, to be learned ever
anew and ever more deeply at the school of Christ and of
the saints of all the ages. Since the Christian liturgy by its
nature is also always a proclamation, we must be people
who are familiar with the Word of God, love it and live

by it: only then can we explain it in an adequate way. "To serve the Lord"—priestly service also means precisely to learn to know the Lord in his Word and to make it known to all those he entrusts to us.

Lastly, two other aspects are part of service. No one is closer to his master than the servant who has access to the most private dimensions of his life. In this sense "to serve" means closeness, it requires familiarity. This familiarity also involves a danger: when we continually encounter the sacred, it risks becoming habitual for us. In this way, reverential fear is extinguished. Conditioned by all our habits, we no longer perceive the great, new and surprising fact that he himself is present, speaks to us, gives himself to us. We must ceaselessly struggle against this becoming accustomed to the extraordinary reality, against the indifference of the heart, always recognizing our insufficiency anew and the grace that there is in the fact that he consigned himself into our hands. To serve means to draw near, but above all it also means obedience. The servant is under the word: "not my will, but thine, be done" (Lk 22:42). With this word Jesus, in the Garden of Olives, has resolved the decisive battle against sin, against the rebellion of the sinful heart. Adam's sin consisted precisely in the fact that he wanted to accomplish his own will and not God's. Humanity's temptation is always to want to be totally autonomous, to follow its own will alone and to maintain that only in this way will we be free; that only thanks to a similarly unlimited freedom would man be completely man. But this is precisely how we pit ourselves against the truth. Because the truth is that we must share our freedom with others and we can be free only in communion with them. This shared freedom can be true freedom only if we enter into what constitutes the very measure of freedom, if we enter into God's will. This fundamental obedience that is part of man ... becomes still more concrete in the priest: we do not preach ourselves, but him and his Word, which we could not have invented ourselves. We proclaim the Word of Christ in the correct way only in communion with his Body. Our obedience is a believing with the Church, a thinking and speaking with the Church, serving through her. What Jesus predicted to Peter also always applies: "You will be taken where you do not want to go." This letting oneself be guided where one does not want to be led is an essential dimension of our service, and it is exactly what makes us free. In this being guided, which can be contrary to our ideas and plans, we experience something new—the wealth of God's love.

"To stand in his presence and serve him": Jesus Christ as the true High Priest of the world has conferred [on] these words a previously unimaginable depth. He, who as Son of God was and is the Lord, has willed to become that Servant of God whom the vision of the *Book of the Prophet Isaiah* had foreseen. He has willed to be the Servant of all. He has portrayed the whole of his high priesthood in the gesture of the washing of the feet. With the gesture of love to the end he washes our dirty feet, with the humility of his service he purifies us from the illness of our pride. Thus, he makes us able to become partakers of God's banquet. He has descended, and the true ascent of man is now accomplished in our descending with him and toward him. His elevation is the Cross. It is the deepest descent and, as love pushed to the end, it is at the same time the culmination of the ascent, the true "elevation" of humanity. "To stand in his presence and serve him": this now means to enter into his call to serve God. The Eucharist as the presence of the descent and ascent of Christ thus always recalls, beyond itself, the many ways of service through love of neighbor. Let us ask the Lord on this day for the gift to be able to say again in this sense our "yes" to his call: "Here am I! Send me" (Is 6:8). Amen.[13]

---

[13] Benedict XVI, Homily for the Chrism Mass, Holy Thursday, March 20, 2008, in Saint Peter's Basilica in Rome, in *Insegnamenti di Benedetto XVI*, vol. 4, pt. 1 (Vatican City: Libreria Editrice Vaticana, 2009), 442–46. [English translation from the Vatican website, lightly emended with reference to the Italian original.]

3. John 17:17: the high-priestly prayer of Jesus, interpretation of priestly ordination

To conclude, I would like to reflect for another moment on several words taken from the high-priestly prayer of Jesus (Jn 17) that, on the eve of my priestly ordination, were particularly engraved on my heart. While the Synoptic Gospels report essentially the preaching of Jesus in Galilee, John—who seems to have had relations of kinship with the Temple aristocracy—relates chiefly the proclamation of Jesus in Jerusalem and mentions questions concerning the Temple and worship. In this context, Jesus' high-priestly prayer (Jn 17) takes on a particular importance.

I do not intend to repeat here the various elements that I analyzed in volume 2 of my book on Jesus,[14] but only to mention the fact that John assumes the spiritual movement of the Letter to the Hebrews, bringing it to completion in his own way. In this sense, notwithstanding all the differences in the exposition, John and the Letter to the Hebrews have the same intention, that is, to show Jesus as true High Priest of the New Covenant. Even the most recent Protestant exegesis agrees extensively on the fact that Jesus, especially in his high-priestly prayer, appears in the act of fulfilling and transforming the ministry of high priest. In this sense, the Letter to the Hebrews and the Gospel of John in the final analysis are equivalent ways of presenting Jesus as High Priest of the New Covenant.

I would like to limit myself only to verses 17 and 18, which especially struck me on the eve of my priestly ordination. Here is the text: "Consecrate them [sanctify them] in the truth; your word is truth. As you sent me into the world, so I have sent them into the world." The term

---

[14] Joseph Ratzinger, *Jesus of Nazareth*, 2:82–102.

"holy" [Latin: *sanctus*] expresses God's particular nature. He alone is the Holy One. Man becomes holy insofar as he begins to be with God. To be with God is to put aside what is only me and to become one with God's whole will. Nevertheless, this liberation from myself can prove to be very painful, and it is never accomplished once and for all. The term "sanctify", however, can also mean very concretely priestly ordination, in the sense in which it implies that the living God radically claims a man for his service. When the text says, "Sanctify [in some translations: consecrate] them in the truth", the Lord is asking the Father to include the Twelve in his mission, to ordain them priests.

"Sanctify them in the truth." It seems that there is also a discreet reference here to the rite of priestly ordination in the Old Testament: the ordinand was in fact physically purified by a complete washing before putting on the sacred vestments. These two elements considered together mean that, in this way, the one sent becomes a new man. But what is a symbolic figure in the ritual of the Old Testament becomes a reality in the prayer of Jesus. The only washing that can really purify men is the truth, is Christ himself. And he is also the new garment to which the exterior cultic vestment alludes. "Sanctify them in the truth." This means: immerse them completely in Jesus Christ so that what Paul noted as the fundamental experience of his apostolate might prove true for them: "It is no longer I who live, but Christ who lives in me" (Gal 2:20).

Thus, on that eve of my ordination, a deep impression was left on my soul of what it truly means to be ordained a priest, beyond all the ceremonial aspects: it means being continually purified and permeated by Christ so that he is the one who speaks and acts in us, and less and less we ourselves. It became clear to me that this process of becoming one with him, and overcoming what is only ours, lasts a whole lifetime and also includes painful liberations and renewals.

In this sense, the words of John 17:17–18 were a signpost for my whole life.

Benedict XVI
Vatican City, Mater Ecclesiae Monastery
September 17, 2019

THE MEANING OF COMMUNION

Historical Forms of the Eucharistic Celebration

In recent centuries, the celebration of the Last Supper has not occupied a central place at all in the ecclesial life of the Protestant churches. In quite a few communities, the Last Supper was celebrated only once a year, on Good Friday. I recall very well a debate with Lutheran-Evangelical theology students that happened in Münster about thirty years ago, during which I pointed out this circumstance. Thereupon a woman pastor present in the group, with great, astounding religious seriousness, tried to defend this practice, presenting it as absolutely reasonable, although at the time it was much less esteemed. It is obvious that, with respect to a practice of this type, the question of inter-communion has no relevance. Only a tangible alignment with everyday Catholic life today can make the question become humanly urgent.

In the early Church, surprisingly, the daily celebration of Holy Mass was very soon considered self-evident. As far as I know, there was no discussion about this practice, which prevailed peacefully. Only in this way can we understand the reason why the mysterious adjective *epiousion* [in the Our Father, Mt 6:11] was almost self-evidently translated as *quotidianus* [daily]. For a Christian, what is

"The Meaning of Communion" was completed on June 28, 2018. Previously unpublished.

supersubstantial is necessary daily. The daily Eucharistic celebration proved to be necessary especially for the presbyters and bishops as "priests" of the New Covenant. The celibate way of life played a significant role in this. Direct, "bodily" contact with the divine mysteries, even in Old Testament times, had played a significant role in ruling out conjugal relations on the days on which the competent priest was responsible for them. However, since now the Christian priest no longer had to deal with the holy mysteries only on occasion but was forever responsible for the Body of the Lord, for the "daily" bread, it became necessary to offer himself completely to him. Later on, from this practice may have developed the idea that, based on the daily Eucharistic celebration throughout the world, all the Masses on earth together were, so to speak, like one constant sacrifice in the Lord's presence, representing the continual presence of the High Priest Jesus Christ in the time and space of the cosmos.

Although in this way, in the Catholic Church, daily celebration of the Eucharist very quickly became the normal way of life for the clergy, the practice of receiving Communion was nevertheless subject to considerable developments for the laity. Certainly, the Sunday precept required that every Catholic participate in the celebration of the mysteries on the Lord's Day, but the Catholic concept of the Eucharist did not necessarily include weekly reception of Communion. I recall that in the era following the Twenties [i.e., 1920s] there were, for the various states of life in the Church, Communion days that as such were also days of confession and thereby came to assume a prominent position even in the life of families. There was a precept to go to confession at least once a year and to receive Communion during the Easter season; added to this were the days of confession and Communion for the Porziuncola indulgence, for the Feast of All Saints, for All Souls' Day, on Christmas, and for the anniversaries that were important for the individual regions (for example, the Feast of Saint Anne for women, that of Our Lady of Sorrows, and so on). These days were characterized by a great religious seriousness in the family and were also days of special preaching. When the farmer, the head of the family, had gone to confession, a special atmosphere reigned in the farmhouse: everyone avoided doing anything that might agitate him and thus endanger his condition of purity in view of the holy mysteries. In those centuries, Holy Communion was not distributed during Holy Mass, but separately, before or after the Eucharistic celebration. A special time was needed for the personal encounter with the Lord, and there did not seem to be room for it during the celebration of the Mass.

But still there were also trends directed toward more frequent Communion that was more connected to the liturgy, and these gained strength with the beginning of the liturgical movement. In my native town, Traunstein, from the late 1930s, we began to notice at Sunday Mass a group of young women and girls who wanted to pray with the words of the liturgy itself, which could be found in a Latin-German missal. Moreover, they pushed for distribution of Communion during the Mass, which at a certain point, after the end of World War II, was also granted to them. It is of course possible to say that in the large European countries there were opposing tendencies, one of which aimed at the reception of Communion weekly or even daily, while the other insisted on the distinction between Eucharistic adoration and the Mass. Subsequently Vatican Council II recognized the good reasons for the first trend and thereby tried to highlight the intrinsic unity between the daily celebration of the Eucharist and personal reception of Communion. At the same time, especially during the war years, on the Lutheran-Evangelical side one could observe a division between the Third Reich and the so-called *deutsche Christen*, German Christians, on the one hand, and the *bekennende Kirche*, the professing Church, on the other. As a result of this division, there was a new agreement between *bekennende Christen*, professing Lutheran Christians, and the Catholic Church. This resulted in a push in favor of shared Eucharistic Communion between the two denominations. In this situation, there was a growing desire for one Body of the Lord, which today, however, runs the risk of losing its strong religious foundation and, in an externalized Church, is defined more by political and social forces than by an interior search for the Lord. In this regard, an image comes to my mind of a Catholic chancellor of the Federal Republic of Germany who, in full view of the television camera and therefore also in view of religiously indifferent persons, drank from the Eucharistic chalice. This gesture, shortly after reunification had taken place, appeared as an essentially political act in which the unity of all Germans became manifest. Even today, when I reflect on this, I notice again very forcefully the alienation of the faith that followed from it. And when presidents of the Federal Republic of Germany, who at the same time were presidents of the synods of their Church, regularly cried out for interconfessional Eucharistic Communion, I see how the request for one bread and one common cup serves other purposes.

Concerning the current situation of Eucharistic life in the Catholic Church, a few remarks may suffice. One very consequential process is the almost complete disappearance of the sacrament of penance, which, following the debate about whether or not collective absolution was sacramental, in practice disappeared in broad sectors of the Church, managing to find a sort of refuge only at the shrines. Meanwhile, nevertheless, various movements and initiatives for the revitalization of the sacrament have arisen, and it is being rediscovered precisely by young people. With the disappearance of the sacrament of penance, a functional concept of the Eucharist spread. Participation appears meaningful only for someone who performs a function within the celebration, for example, the lector or the extraordinary minister of Communion. Those who are present at the Eucharist, understood purely as a meal, obviously receive also the gift of the Eucharist. In a situation like this, where the understanding of the Eucharist has been protestantized to a great extent, intercommunion appears natural. On the other hand, though, the Catholic understanding of the Eucharist has not vanished entirely, and above all the World Youth Days have brought about a rediscovery of Eucharistic adoration and, thus, also of the Lord's presence in the sacrament.

Theological Aspects

Protestant exegesis keeps going farther, affirming the opinion that the Last Supper of Jesus had been prepared by the Master's so-called "meals with sinners" and could be understood only on the basis of them. But that is not the case. The offering of the Body and Blood of Jesus Christ is not directly connected to his meals with sinners. Independently of the question whether or not the Last Supper of Jesus was a Paschal meal, it is situated in the theological and legal tradition of the Feast of Passover. Consequently, it is closely connected to the family, to the household, and to membership in the people of Israel. In keeping with this prescription, Jesus celebrated Passover with his family, in other words, with the apostles, who had become his new family. In this way, he obeyed a precept whereby the pilgrims who went to Jerusalem could join in groups, the so-called *khaburot*. Christians continued this tradition. They are his *khaburah*, his family, which he formed out of his band of pilgrims who travel with him the road of the Gospel through the realm of history.[15] Thus celebrating the Eucharist in the early Church was connected from the beginning with the community of believers and thus with rigorous conditions for admittance, as we can see from the most ancient sources: *Didache*, Justin Martyr, etc.[16] This has nothing to do with slogans like "inclusive Church" or "exclusive Church"; rather, the fact that the Church profoundly becomes one thing, one Body with the Lord, is presupposed, so that she can forcefully bring his life and his light into the world.

In the ecclesial communities that sprang from the Reformation, celebrations of the sacrament are called "the Lord's Supper". In the Catholic Church, the celebration of the sacrament of the Body and Blood of Christ is called "the Eucharist". This is not an accidental, purely linguistic distinction; rather, the distinction between the titles manifests a profound difference bound up with their understanding of the sacrament itself. The well-known Protestant theologian Edmund Schlink, in a speech listened to by many during the council, declared that he could not recognize the Lord's institution in the Catholic celebration

---

[15] See Joseph Ratzinger, *Schauen auf den Durchbohrten* (Einsiedeln: Johannes Verlag, 1984), 88; English translation by Graham Harrison, *Behold the Pierced One* (San Francisco: Ignatius Press, 1986), 74–76.

[16] See *Catechism of the Catholic Church*, nos. 1136ff. and 1345ff.

of the Eucharist. With that he obviously meant that the Catholic Mass, as it is celebrated, bears no resemblance to the Last Supper of Jesus. In his view, the totally different way of celebrating already makes evident the non-identity between the Catholic liturgy of the Mass and the Lord's Supper. And thus the detachment of Catholicism from the institution of Jesus becomes manifest. He was obviously convinced that Luther, by returning to the pure structure of the Last Supper, had overcome the Catholic falsification and had visibly reestablished fidelity to the Lord's command, "Do this ..."

It is not necessary to discuss here what in the meantime has become an established fact, namely, that from a purely historical perspective, the Last Supper of Jesus was altogether different from a celebration of the Lutheran Supper. On the other hand, it is correct to remark that even the primitive Church did not repeat the Last Supper phenomenologically, but rather, instead of the evening Supper, deliberately celebrated in the morning the encounter with the Lord, which even in the earliest times was no longer called a Supper, but Eucharist. Only in the encounter with the Risen Lord on the morning of the first day is the institution of the Eucharist complete, because only with the living Christ can the sacred mysteries be celebrated.

What happened here? Why did the nascent Church act in this way?

Let us turn again for a moment to the Supper and to the institution of the Eucharist by Jesus during the Supper. When the Lord said, "Do this," he did not mean to invite his disciples to repeat the Last Supper as such. If it was a Passover celebration, it is clear that, in keeping with the precepts of the Exodus, Passover was celebrated once a year and could not be repeated several times during the year. But even independently of this, it is obvious that no command was given to repeat the entire Supper eaten on that occasion, but rather solely the new offering of Jesus in which, in keeping with the words of institution, the tradition of Sinai is connected with the proclamation of the New Covenant to which Jeremiah in particular testified. The Church, knowing that she was bound by the words "Do this", therefore knew at the same time that the Supper as a whole was not supposed to be repeated, but that she needed to extrapolate what was essentially new and that in this way a new comprehensive form would be found.

Twentieth-century Catholic liturgists erred when they tried to deduce the form of the Eucharistic meal as a whole from the institution of the Eucharist in the context of a Passover meal. The most ancient account of the celebration of the Eucharist that we have available—the one handed down to us by Justin Martyr around the year 155—already shows that a new unity had formed, consisting of two fundamental components: the encounter with the Word of God in a liturgy of the Word and then the "Eucharist" as *logiké latreia* [Rom 12:1, "spiritual worship"]. "Eucharist" is the translation of the Hebrew word *berakah* (thanksgiving) and designates the central core of the Hebrew faith and prayer in Jesus' time. The texts on the Last Supper tell us at length that Jesus "gave thanks with a prayer of blessing", and therefore the Eucharist, together with the offering of the bread and wine, should be considered the core of the form of his Last Supper. In particular, J. A. Jungmann and Louis Bouyer were the ones who pointed out the meaning of *Eucharistia* as a constitutive element.

When the celebration of what Jesus instituted in the context of the Last Supper is called Eucharist, this term validly expresses both obedience to the institution of Jesus and the new form of sacrament that developed in the

encounter with the Risen Lord. It is meant as a repro-
duction, not of the Last Supper of Jesus, but of the new
event of the encounter with the Risen Lord: novelty and
fidelity stand together. The difference between the des-
ignations "Supper" and "Eucharist" is not superficial and
accidental, but rather indicates a fundamental difference in
understanding Jesus' command.

In one authoritative German-language work of academic
literature in the field of liturgy on the Holy Eucharist,[17]
in the accurately elaborated description of how the form
of the Eucharist came to develop, the Cross of Christ does
not appear. Once when I expressed my surprise about this
to a well-known German liturgist, he explained to me that
the crucifixion of Jesus was certainly not a liturgical act
and that therefore it had no place in the history of the
liturgy. Even though this formalistic view of the development of the liturgical celebration is quite understandable,
it nevertheless tends to obscure its essential foundation.
When at the Last Supper the Lord says: "This is my body",
"this is my blood", these two decisive expressions can be
understood only in reference to the gift of himself that
will take place on the Cross. No doubt Jesus, on the one
hand, stands amid the disciples; on the other hand, he
explains these offerings as Body and Blood that are given
to them. These words of institution make sense only as
an anticipation of an event and thus create an inseparable
unity between the event in the Cenacle and the transformation of his slaying into a gift. These two expressions
have meaning only if at that instant Jesus anticipated in an
absolutely real way his Cross and Resurrection. The words

---

[17] Hans Bernhard Meyer, S.J., *Eucharistie* (Regensburg: Verlag Friedrich Pustet, 1989).

pronounced in the Upper Room therefore cannot be separated from the event that is the real reason why they are
pronounced and without which they would be meaningless. They show us that Jesus did not take upon himself his
torment simply as an unavoidable disgrace, but rather he
accepted his slaying in advance; and what was a criminal
act on the part of the executioners, he for his part transformed into an act of love that as such then conquered
even death, becoming Resurrection. And so this process of
transforming death into love is present in every celebration
of the Eucharist and with it the new modality of sacrifice
that includes all the currents of the Old Covenant and in a
way the secret expectation of all religions.[18]

When the Lord says to his disciples, "Do this ...", he
announces the totality that the Letter to the Hebrews presents as the content of the Eucharistic event in terms of the
Temple worship. In other words: Eucharist is not only a
distribution of offerings or just a "meal", but embraces the
whole reality of redemption; it is true "worship". In reality,
this is precisely the authentic, profound difference between
the concept of Jesus' command that developed with the
Reformation and the Catholic faith in the Eucharist. In
the Reformers' interpretations, the Eucharist is solely a meal,
in the radical sense whereby only the sacred offering is distributed and given to be eaten, while for the Catholic faith
in the Eucharist, the entire process of Jesus' gift in his death
and Resurrection is present, a process without which these
offerings could not exist. Body and Blood are not things
that can be distributed; rather, they are the person of Jesus
Christ who offers himself. For this reason, participation in a

---

[18] See my book *The Spirit of the Liturgy*, trans. John Saward (San Francisco:
Ignatius Press, 2000), 35–50, and the related passages in my book *Jesus of Nazareth*, 2:103–44.

Holy Mass always has meaning for all Catholics, even when they—for whatever reasons—are unable or unwilling to "eat" the sacred offering. Participation in Holy Mass, even without receiving Communion, has an absolutely reasonable meaning from a Catholic perspective, while from the Protestant viewpoint, it is meaningless. From this vantage point, one understands the Protestants' insistence on intercommunion. If they take part in the "Supper" without eating, their presence has no meaning. For a Catholic, participation in Communion is not equally mandatory. Even without eating, he takes part in the event of Jesus' gift, which is present in the sacrament.

All this, finally, gives rise to another fundamental question: What, in reality, is the offering of the Supper or, respectively, of the celebration of the Mass? Those on the Catholic side ought to recognize more clearly and gratefully the fact that Luther, with his characteristic passion, firmly maintained the Real Presence of the Body and Blood of Christ, unlike Zwingli and Calvin. Following discussions about the Supper with the other Reformers, he reportedly said that he preferred to accept all the horrors of the papacy rather than to join together with those who disputed the Real Presence. For this reason, the 1973 "Concord of Leuenberg", by which all the communities that sprang from the Reformation joined in table fellowship, was for the Lutherans a step of decisive importance. It is still surprising, of course, to see how obvious this step seemed, practically speaking, even though it abandoned the Lutheran tradition on one essential point.

One gets the impression that in broad sectors of the Reformed churches, they believe that what was possible for the Lutherans can no longer be impossible even for the Catholics.

Even though Luther's fidelity to the Real Presence must certainly be acknowledged, it is nevertheless important to analyze carefully his idea of the Real Presence, which as such, however, fundamentally conflicts with the Catholic concept. While the Catholic Church together with the Orthodox Churches teaches the transubstantiation (*metousíosis*) of bread and wine, Luther rejects this metaphysical formula and affirms consubstantiation instead. In other words: while for Catholics a transformation of the offerings occurs, as a result of which they are no longer bread and wine but the Body and Blood of Jesus Christ, for Luther there is no transformation. He insists on the unquestionably real impression that they continue to be bread and wine and are tasted by us as such. But together with the bread and wine ("in, with, and under" the offerings) the Lord becomes present, his Body and his Blood. The offerings as such are not transformed, but to them is added the presence of the Lord. This, however, means also that the presence is only temporary, in other words, limited to the celebration and to one part of it. After the celebration, what had been added solely for the reception of Communion ceases, and what remains of the offerings is again profane, as it was before, so that the bread and wine, for example, do not have to be preserved as sacred species, but can be used again in everyday life, as before.

Corresponding to the idea that the celebration of the Supper involves no transformation—but that the Body and Blood of Christ, like any other things, are added to the bread and wine—is a concept of the essence of Christian life that certainly constitutes the most profound difference between the Protestant interpretation of being Christian and the tradition of the Catholic faith. It is expressed in the formula *simul iustus et peccator* [at the same time just and a sinner]: becoming a Christian does not change man but only adds something else to him.

In the term "transubstantiation", the whole emphasis is on the "trans-": in the Eucharist a transformation occurs, a transformation that goes to the very depths of being, just as becoming Christian requires of a human person a fundamental change of his being, precisely a *conversio*. From this perspective, it is inevitable that the [Protestant] concept of sacramental Communion is fundamentally different, too: for the Lutheran tradition, the "Body of Christ" is eaten along with the bread, while in the Catholic view, Christ is taken and received in his sacrificial gift, and thus we allow ourselves to be drawn into this very gift.

In Luther's system, the Cross does not become present in the Eucharist, but the Body and Blood of Christ are eaten only in the bread and wine. There is a profound reason for this conception: sacrifice is an institution that belongs to the Law and, therefore, must be judged negatively. For Luther, in the Law God acts *sub contrario*, as though he were his own adversary. With that, Luther adopts the position of Marcion: the Law is anti-God. And nevertheless Luther, unlike Marcion, whose judgment on the Law he shares, acknowledges it as Scripture, and this means that he situates within the Bible the conflict between faith and the promise, making God act against himself in the Bible itself. Luther's subtle Marcionism, which theologically explains and establishes his radical aversion to the Jews also, is the authentic problem in his interpretation of Sacred Scripture. In contrast, the Catholic tradition from the beginning considered the Law and the Gospel to be not contradictory, but profoundly correlative. The difficulty in understanding correctly the Catholic faith and in interpreting it in a profound unity with

Sacred Scripture can be traced back to two elements of modern thought:

—the crisis of the concept of "substance" compromises the philosophical foundation of the Catholic interpretation;

—exegesis that seeks to be rigidly historical confines the Old Testament to the past and does not have the tools to explain the dynamic of the passageways through which the past opens up into the present and the future.

Catholic theology today and tomorrow will have to continue to work on these two points. And yet the essential vision of what is Catholic can be recognized clearly in its reasoning, even without satisfactory intellectual tools, as it should have become clear from the preceding reflections.

But what happens to the bread and wine in the celebration of the Holy Eucharist? Something is not added to them temporarily, but rather bread and wine are snatched away from the things of this world so as to enter into the new world of the risen Jesus Christ. Just as the Risen Lord did not simply return, like Lazarus or one of the others who was brought back to life, for a certain time to this life, but rather belongs to the new world of the Resurrection, so too it happens with the offerings of bread and wine. To use an image, we can say that something like nuclear fission happens, by means of which the Body of Jesus lives again in a new way. Something like this event occurs in the Eucharistic transformation: bread and wine are no longer created realities of this world that consist in themselves, but rather are bearers of the mysteriously real form of the Risen Lord.

In order to explain this, the philosophical category of "substance" was employed, saying that the substance is taken away, as noted, and replaced with another, while the accidents of the bread and wine remain. Over the course of the development of philosophical thought and of the natural sciences, the concept of substance changed essentially and, likewise, the concept of what, in Aristotelian thought, had been designated as an "accident". The concept of substance, which previously had been applied to every reality that subsists in itself, was more and more often used to refer to what is physically ungraspable, such as molecules, atoms, or elementary particles—although today we know that even these are not ultimately "substances", but rather structures of relations. This gave rise to a new task for Christian philosophy. The fundamental category of all reality in general terms is no longer substance but, rather, relation. In this regard, we Christians can say only that for our faith God himself is relation, *relatio subsistens*. The fundamental category of a philosophy that corresponds to the findings of today's natural sciences is identical to the fundamental category of the faith: God is *relatio subsistens*.

From this perspective, we should seek to understand in a new way what "transformation of the substance" means. But even prescinding from hypothetical new conceptual explanations of this sort, it is fundamentally clear that in the Holy Eucharist a little flesh and a little blood are not added to the bread and wine, but rather the offerings are now bearers of the dynamic of the crucified and risen Christ. Indeed, again in the Holy Eucharist one does not receive a little of the Body and a little of the Blood of Jesus, but rather one enters into the dynamic of the love of Jesus Christ that takes concrete form in the Cross and the Resurrection and becomes really present. This is very important also for a correct Eucharistic devotion. The question "What do I receive?" needs to be answered: I let myself be taken up by the Lord Jesus Christ into the dynamic of his person, which became flesh, and inserted into the new world of the Resurrection. The personalism of the Christian faith and the vast extent of its dynamic show the way for a correct Eucharistic devotion. Part of it, therefore, is sacrifice, not as something contrary to God or as the attempt to render a service by a human work, but rather as the way in which Christ opens the door to God and thereby redeems us.

Finally, another essential aspect should be analyzed: To whom is it granted to preside at that sacred celebration? For the Lutheran tradition, as a matter of principle any Christian can do this, but in order to maintain good order normally the pastor alone does it, since by his profession he is appointed a leader for this purpose. For the Catholic tradition, in contrast, the service of the man who presides, who at the canon recites the words of transformation, is bound up with the sacrament of priestly ordination. Only someone who has allowed himself to be taken by the Lord into this service through the Church, and has been con- secrated to preside at the Eucharist, can perform the ser- vice of the transformation, which as such is always ordered to the great transformation of the entire creation. Paul described his mission with these words: "On some points I have written to you very boldly by way of reminder, because of the grace given me by God to be a minister of Christ Jesus to the Gentiles in the priestly service of the gospel of God, so that the offering of the Gentiles may be acceptable, sanctified by the Holy Spirit" (Rom 15:15–17).

What Is at Stake

Let us try, finally, to summarize very briefly what is at stake.

Transubstantiation, not consubstantiation, means transformation, *conversio*, and not merely addition. This statement extends well beyond the offerings and tells us fundamentally what Christianity is: it is a transformation of our life, a transformation of the world as a whole into a new existence. If Christ said to Mary Magdalene, "Do not hold me, for I have not yet ascended to the Father" (Jn 20:17), this signifies that being Christian means a dynamic of ascent; it is participation in Jesus Christ's new way of existing. Christ did not return to the human life that preceded his death and is known to us, but rather became a new reality that draws us into its newness.

Transubstantiation and consubstantiation are philosophical concepts that, in our opinion, may not belong to the heart of the faith. On the basis of his rejection of philosophy, Luther had been unable to accept transubstantiation, creating in its place the apparently harmless model of consubstantiation that, nevertheless, in an altogether obvious way is not proportioned to the reality of the gift given to us by the Lord.

Here, in my opinion, it is important to consider the other great philosophical term that the Fathers of Nicaea used to express the newness and the difference of the faith in Jesus Christ in comparison to all that had been thought until then: *homoousios*. In reality, this is not a bit of philosophical tinsel that is foreign to the faith and causes alienation, but rather the way of receiving it completely in itself, in its difference and newness; this happens in a similar way with the term "transubstantiation". What is expressed in this way is the radicality of what happened and of what happens in Christ and starting from Christ. This led to difficult times when classical physics connected the concept of substance to fixed ultimate units of reality. Today, however, it has become clear that reality does not ultimately consist of supporting elements, but should be imagined as having the form of rays. Being is relation. Recently a physicist summarized the situation this way: "The classic doctrine of the Eucharist was persuaded of the fact that 'reality' and 'quantity' do not coincide..., but that the reality is of an essentially different type, and nevertheless is 'reality' anyway."[19] The non-identification of reality and quantity is the nucleus of the theological statement, which can continue to exist even in view of physics. Transubstantiation is not a philosophical alienation of the faith that has become untenable in a new situation of our knowledge about matter, but rather is an expression of the unheard-of and new thing that has become possible with the anticipation of the Resurrection in the Cenacle: the inclusion of a piece of this matter in Jesus Christ's new way of being.

This means that Eucharist does not signify only a meal shared by Christians after the Resurrection, in which they would eat a bit of the Body of Christ and would drink a bit of his Blood. What this might reasonably signify is then truly difficult to say. The remarkable Eucharistic event goes farther: it is a presence of the living Christ, a participation in his death and Resurrection. Holy Mass makes present the sacrifice of the Cross. Luther condemned this in the harshest way, on the basis of his rejection of the concept of sacrifice. And nevertheless it is the sole reasonable interpretation of the Eucharist that was instituted on the evening before the Passion; and it is, finally, the gift of right worship, for which the history of religions yearned, and particularly the history of Israel. Odo Casel presented this concept of the Eucharist in a way that is correct and yet

---

[19] Rudolf Hilfer, "Transsubstantiation: Zur Naturphilosophie der eucharistischen Wandlung", *Forum Katholische Theologie* 33/4 (2017): 303–18, at 306.

one-sided, especially because he lacked an understanding
of the Old Testament development and tried to explain
the Eucharist solely in terms of the worship of the Greek
mystery religions. To arrive in this field at an understanding that is in keeping with the Scriptures and to develop
Eucharistic theology adequately is a fine challenge for the
theology of tomorrow.

This sort of understanding of the Holy Eucharist also
presupposes, nevertheless, the early Church's concept of
Church, or the Catholic concept of Church. While for
Luther the Church as such becomes a reality only from
time to time in the communal assemblies, the words of
Jesus and the preaching of the apostles presuppose the
Church as a community that, with full authority derived
from the Lord, in other words, from the sacrament, can do
what no community could do and would be authorized to
do by its own power. The celebration of the Eucharist is
possible solely with the full power conferred by the sacrament, which alone can enable the consecrated man to
pronounce the words of transformation of the *Eucharistia*.

If we consider these correlations, we can note with
gratitude that in the past century a new and far-reaching
point of departure has been given to us, from the ecumen-
ical perspective, too, for a more in-depth theology of the
Eucharist, which certainly still must be further contemplated, experienced, and suffered. Fortunately, the Magisterium of the Church has already taken several important
steps toward a more in-depth understanding of the Eucharist, beyond the decree on the Eucharist of the Council
of Trent. In the first place, the liturgical reform of Vatican II—the beginnings of which had already been put
in place by Pius XII with the renewal of the liturgy of
the Easter Vigil—is also a step toward a deeper theological

understanding of the Eucharist. The *Catechism of the Catholic Church* (nos. 1322–1419), published in 1992, sets forth the teaching of the Church on the Holy Eucharist in its entirety. Finally, John Paul II dedicated his last encyclical, *Ecclesia de Eucharistia* (2003), to the theme of the Eucharist and the Church. Today the Church must face a major task. Authentic *ecumenism* can come about only by facing the major questions with which the Lord confronts us in his Paschal Mystery and by arduously and personally processing them. And from this point of departure, the correct paths for true ecumenism become evident, also.

Chapter Five

TOPICS FROM MORAL THEOLOGY

THE CHURCH AND THE SCANDAL
OF SEXUAL ABUSE

On February 21 to 24, at the invitation of Pope Francis, the presidents of all the bishops' conferences in the world gathered at the Vatican to discuss the current crisis of the faith and of the Church—a crisis felt throughout the world after distressing revelations of clerical abuse against minors. The extent and gravity of the reported incidents have deeply distressed priests and lay people alike, leading more than a few to call into question the very faith of the Church. Here, a strong signal and a new beginning were necessary in order to render the Church truly credible again as a light of the nations and as a helping force against the powers of destruction.

Since I myself served in a position of responsibility as shepherd of the Church at the moment of the public outbreak of the crisis, as well as during its escalation, I could not help wondering what I, looking at the past, could contribute to this new beginning—even though, as pope emeritus, I no longer had any direct responsibility. Thus, after the meeting of the presidents of the bishops' conferences was announced, I compiled some notes in order to make a suggestion or two that might help in this difficult

Pope Emeritus Benedikt XVI, "Die Kirche und der Skandal des sexuellen Missbrauchs", *Klerusblatt* 99/4 (2019): 75–81. The text was published in Italian at the website of *Il Corriere della Sera* on April 12, 2019. English translation by A. C. Wimmer, edited by Ignatius Press to conform to the Italian edition of *What Is Christianity?*

hour. After contacts with Secretary of State Pietro Cardinal Parolin and the Holy Father [Pope Francis] himself, I think it is appropriate to publish this text in the *Klerusblatt* ["Clergy Journal", a monthly periodical for clergy in Bavaria].

My work is divided into three parts.

In the first, I attempt to outline very briefly the social context of the question, without which the problem cannot be understood. I try to show that in the 1960s an unheard-of event took place that, in its scale, was almost unprecedented in history. One could say that in the twenty years from 1960 to 1980, the normative standards on sexuality that had been in force until then collapsed entirely, and a new absence of norms arose that many people have since worked hard to remedy.

In the second part, I try to indicate the effects of this situation on priestly formation and on the lives of priests.

Finally, in the third part, I develop some perspectives for a proper response on the part of the Church.

Moral Theology and the Sixties

The situation started with the state-mandated and state-financed introduction of children and young people to the nature of sexuality. In Germany, the then–Minister of Health, Käte Strobel, commissioned an educational film showcasing everything that until that time could not be shown in public, including sexual intercourse. Then what at first had been intended only for the sexual education of young people subsequently was accepted as a regular possibility, as though it were obvious.

The *Sexkoffer* issued by the Austrian government [a controversial "suitcase" of sex education materials used in

Austrian schools in the late 1980s] had similar effects. Sexual and pornographic films then became such an everyday reality that they were screened at discount theaters [*Bahnhofskinos*]. I still remember walking through the city of Regensburg one day and seeing crowds of people standing and waiting in front of a big movie theater—a phenomenon that until then had been seen only during wartime [at groceries and dry goods stores] when some special ration was expected. Also engraved on my memory is arriving in the city on Good Friday in 1970 and seeing all the news kiosks plastered with a large poster of two completely naked people in a tight embrace.

Among the freedoms that the Revolution of 1968 intended to gain was complete sexual freedom, one which no longer admitted any norms. The propensity for violence that characterized these years was closely linked to this spiritual collapse. In fact, showing sex films was no longer allowed on airplanes, since violent behavior would break out among the little community of passengers. Because the excesses in clothing styles likewise provoked aggression, school administrators tried to introduce school uniforms that might foster a climate of learning.

It must be mentioned that among the features of the Revolution of 1968 was the fact that even pedophilia was proclaimed as permissible and appropriate. For the young people in the Church, at least, but not only for them, this was in many ways a very difficult time. I have always wondered how young people in this situation could approach and accept the priesthood, with all its consequences. All these developments resulted in a sharp decline in priestly vocations during those years and an upsurge in laicizations.

At the same time, independently of this phenomenon, Catholic moral theology suffered a collapse that rendered

the Church defenseless against these developments in society. I will try to outline very briefly the trajectory of this
dynamic. Until the Second Vatican Council, Catholic
moral theology was broadly founded on natural law, with
Sacred Scripture cited only for background or substantia-
tion. In the council's struggle for a new understanding of
revelation, the natural law option was almost completely
set aside, and a moral theology based entirely on the Bible
was demanded.

I still remember how the Jesuit faculty in Frankfurt had
one highly gifted young priest (Bruno Schüller) lay the
groundwork for developing a morality based entirely on
Scripture. Father Schüller's fine dissertation shows the first
step in the elaboration of a morality founded on Scripture. Father Schüller was then sent to the United States
for further studies and came back with the realization that
morality could not be systematically presented on the basis
of the Bible alone. He then attempted to develop a more
pragmatic moral theology, without, however, managing
to provide a response to the crisis of morality.

Finally, the thesis that morality should be defined exclusively on the basis of the purposes of human action was
widely accepted. The old adage "the end justifies the
means" was not confirmed in quite so crude a form, and
yet the concept contained in it had become decisive. Consequently, there could no longer be anything absolutely
good, much less anything categorically evil, but only rel-
ative value judgments. There was no longer the good,
but only what was relatively better at the moment and
depending on the circumstances.

In the late 1980s and the '90s, the crisis of justifying
and presenting Catholic morality assumed dramatic proportions. On January 5, 1989, the "Cologne Declaration" was published, signed by fifteen Catholic professors

of theology. It focused on various critical points in the relationship between the episcopal teaching office and the task of theology. This document, which at first did not go beyond the usual level of protests, nevertheless grew very rapidly into an outcry against the Magisterium of the Church, rallying in a very visible and audible way the potential opposition that was forming throughout the world against the expected Magisterial documents by John Paul II.[1]

John Paul II, who knew the situation of moral theology very well and followed it closely, commissioned work on an encyclical to set these things right again. It was published with the title *Veritatis splendor* on August 6, 1993, triggering vehement backlashes on the part of moral theologians. Already before this there had been the *Catechism of the Catholic Church*, which had systematically and persuasively presented the morality taught by the Church.

I cannot forget how Franz Böckle—then among the leading German-speaking moral theologians, who after becoming a professor emeritus had retired to his native Switzerland—made an announcement in anticipation of the judgments possibly contained in *Veritatis splendor*. He said that if the document should determine that there are actions that are always and under all circumstances to be classified as evil, he would speak out against it with all his might. The Good Lord spared him from carrying out his resolution; Böckle died on July 8, 1991. The encyclical was published on August 6, 1993, and did indeed include the statement that there are actions that can never become good. The pope was fully aware of the weight of this decision at that moment and, specifically for this part

[1] See Dietmar Mieth, "Kölner Erklärung", in *Lexikon für Theologie und Kirche* VI, 3rd ed. (1997).

of his text, he had once again consulted leading specialists who had not participated in the drafting of the encyclical. There could not and must not be any doubt that the morality founded on the principle of weighing goods must respect a final boundary. There are goods that are never subject to such a calculus. There are values that can never legitimately be sacrificed for the sake of a still higher value; they have priority even over the preservation of physical life. There is martyrdom. God is greater even than physical survival. A life that is saved at the price of denying God, a life based on an ultimate lie, is a non-life. Martyrdom is a fundamental category of Christian existence. Basically it is no longer morally necessary, in the theory advocated by Böckle and many others, and this shows that the very essence of Christianity is at stake in this dispute.

In moral theology, of course, another question had meanwhile become pressing. A certain thesis had gained widespread acceptance, namely, that the Magisterium of the Church should have final and definitive competence ("infallibility") only in matters of faith, while questions of morality could not become a matter for infallible decisions of the Church's Magisterium. There is of course something correct in this thesis that merits further in-depth discussion. Nevertheless, there is a moral minimum that is inseparably linked to the fundamental decision of faith and must be defended if faith is not to be reduced to a theory. For this reason, the claim that faith makes with regard to everyday life must be acknowledged. It becomes clear from all this how radically the Church's authority in moral matters is being called into question. Whoever denies the Church's final doctrinal competence in this domain forces her to remain silent precisely at the point where the boundary between truth and falsehood is at stake.

Independently of this question, a thesis developed in many sectors of moral theology that the Church does not and cannot have her own morality. In arguing this, it was emphasized that all moral propositions would have equivalents in other religions, too, and therefore a Christian *proprium* [a distinctively Christian morality] could not exist. However, the question of the *proprium* of a biblical morality is not answered by saying that for every single proposition, an equivalent can be found somewhere in other religions. Rather, biblical morality as a whole is what is new and different compared to its individual parts.

The particular feature of the moral teaching of Sacred Scripture lies ultimately in the fact that it is anchored to the image of God, in faith in the one God who manifested himself in Jesus Christ and lived as a man. The Decalogue is an application to human life of biblical faith in God. The image of God and morality belong together, and thus they produce what is specifically new in the Christian attitude toward the world and human life. Moreover, Christianity has been described from the beginning with the word *hodós* [Greek: "road"]. Faith is a path, a way to live. In the early Church, the catechumenate was instituted as a living space set apart from an increasingly depraved culture, a space in which what was specific and new about the Christian way of life was taught and, at the same time, safeguarded against the common way of living. I think that even today something like catechumenal communities is necessary, so that Christian life in its distinctive character can be affirmed.

Initial Reactions in the Church

As I have tried to show, the unraveling of the Christian understanding of morality—an ongoing process that was long in preparation—reached an unprecedented degree of radicality in the 1960s. This confusion concerning the

Church's teaching authority in matters of morality necessarily had repercussions on the various spheres of ecclesial
life, also. In the context of the meeting of episcopal conference presidents from across the world with Pope Francis
[February 21–24, 2019, at the Vatican], the question of
priestly life and seminary formation is especially crucial.
With regard to the issue of preparation for the priestly
ministry in the seminaries, one can indeed note a widespread breakdown of the existing form of this preparation.

In various seminaries, homosexual cliques were formed
that acted more or less openly and that markedly changed
the climate in these seminaries. In one seminary in south-
ern Germany, candidates for the priesthood lived together
with candidates for the lay pastoral ministry. At the common meals, seminarians ate together with the lay pastors—
who were sometimes accompanied by their wives and
children and in some cases by their fiancées. The climate
in this seminary could not foster priestly formation. The
Holy See knew about these problems, without having
detailed information. As a first step, an Apostolic Visitation
to the seminaries in the United States was ordered.

Since the criteria for the selection and appointment of
bishops had likewise been changed after Vatican II, the
relationship of bishops to their seminaries was also very
different. Now the main criterion for the appointment
of new bishops was considered to be their "conciliarity",
a term that of course could be understood to mean very
different things. In many parts of the Church, the conciliar attitude was in fact understood as a critical or negative
approach to the hitherto existing tradition, which now
had to be replaced by a new, radically open relationship
with the world. One bishop, who had previously been
a seminary rector, arranged for pornographic films to be
shown to the seminarians, presumably with the intention

of thereby making them able to resist behavior contrary to the faith. There were individual bishops—not only in the United States—who rejected the Catholic tradition altogether and aimed to cultivate in their dioceses a kind of new, modern "Catholicity". Perhaps it is worth mentioning that, in not a few seminaries, students caught reading my books were considered unsuitable for the priesthood. My books were hidden away like naughty literature and read only surreptitiously, so to speak.

The Apostolic Visitation that took place at this point brought no new findings, apparently because various forces had formed a coalition to conceal the real situation. A second visitation was ordered, which brought to light considerably more information but, on the whole, failed to achieve any results. In spite of this, since the 1970s the situation in seminaries has generally improved. Still, a strengthening of priestly vocations came about only sporadically, because the overall situation had taken a different turn.

The question of pedophilia, as far as I recall, did not become acute until the second half of the 1980s. By then, it had already grown to become a public issue in the United States, to the point where the bishops sought help in Rome, because canon law, as established in the new [1983] code, did not seem to be an adequate basis for taking the necessary measures. At first Rome and the Roman canonists had difficulties with these concerns; in their opinion, temporary suspension from priestly ministry ought to suffice to bring about purification and clarification. This could not be accepted by the American bishops, because this meant that the priests would remain in the service of the bishop and thus could be considered directly associated with him. A renewal and deepening of criminal law, which had deliberately been framed loosely in the new code, could move ahead only at a slow pace.

In addition, there was a fundamental problem that concerned the concept of criminal law. By now only so-called *garantismo* ["guarantism", a kind of procedural protectionism, featured in the Italian constitution] was regarded as "conciliar". This means that above all else the rights of the accused had to be guaranteed, to the point where conviction was excluded in practice. As a counterweight to the often inadequate defense options available to accused theologians, their right to defense was extended so much along the lines of *garantismo* that convictions became almost impossible.

Allow me a brief excursus at this point. Given the extent of the crimes of pedophilia, a saying of Jesus comes to mind: "Whoever causes one of these little ones who believe in me to sin, it would be better for him if a great millstone were hung round his neck and he were thrown into the sea" (Mk 9:42). However, in its original sense, this saying does not refer to the luring of children for sexual purposes. Instead, the phrase "little ones", in Jesus' language, means simple believers who might be shaken in their faith by the intellectual pride of those who consider themselves intelligent. Here, then, Jesus is protecting the good of the faith with an emphatic threat of punishment for those who do it harm. Although the modern application of these words to refer specifically to child abuse is not incorrect, this reading must not obscure their original meaning. Contrary to any *garantismo*, this original sense makes it quite clear that it is not only the right of the accused that matters and needs to be guaranteed. Other precious goods, such as the faith, are just as important.

Therefore, although respect for the defendant is a good protected by law, a balanced canon law that corresponds to Jesus' message in its entirety must provide guarantees not only in favor of the accused. It must also protect the faith, which likewise is an important good protected by law. A correctly formulated canon law must thus contain a two-fold guarantee: legal protection of the accused and legal protection of the good that is at stake. Nowadays when someone proposes this self-evident notion, the words generally fall on deaf ears, and one meets with indifference about protecting the faith legally. In the current understanding of right and wrong [*Rechtsbewußtsein*], the faith no longer seems to have the status of a good to be protected. This is an alarming situation that the pastors of the Church must bear in mind and take seriously.

Adding to these brief notes on the situation of priestly formation at the time of the public outbreak of the crisis, I would now like to make a few remarks about the development of canon law on this matter. In principle, the Congregation for the Clergy is responsible for dealing with crimes committed by priests. However, since *garantismo* largely prevailed at the time, we agreed with Pope John Paul II that it was appropriate to assign the competence for these offenses to the Congregation for the Doctrine of the Faith, under the title *Delicta maiora contra fidem* ["Major offenses against the faith"].

This arrangement also made it possible to impose the maximum penalty, in other words, reduction to the lay state, which, on the other hand, could not have been imposed under other legal provisions. This was not a ploy so as to be able to impose the maximum penalty, but rather a consequence of the gravity of the faith for the Church.

Indeed, it is important to keep in mind that such crimes by clerics ultimately damage the faith: such offenses are possible only when faith no longer determines man's actions. The severity of the punishment, however, also presupposes a clear proof of the offense committed—this is the substance of *garantismo* that remains in force. In other words, in order to impose the maximum penalty lawfully, a genuine criminal process is required. Yet this requirement overwhelmed both the dioceses and the Holy See. And so we established a minimal form of a criminal trial and left open the eventuality that the Holy See itself would take over the trial if the diocese or the metropolitan administration was unable to conduct it. In each case, the trial would have to be reviewed by the Congregation for the Doctrine of the Faith in order to guarantee the rights of the accused. Finally, in the Feria IV (i.e., the plenary assembly of the congregation), we created an appellate court to provide also for the possibility of an appeal. Because all of this really went beyond the capacities of the Congregation for the Doctrine of the Faith, and because delays occurred that had to be prevented, given the nature of the matter, Pope Francis has since undertaken further reforms.

Several Prospects

What should we do? Must we create another Church in order to set things right? Well, that experiment has already been made and has already failed. Only obedience to our Lord Jesus Christ and love for him can show us the right way. Therefore, let us try first and foremost to understand in a new and interior way what the Lord wanted and wants from us.

First, I would say that, if we really wanted to summarize as succinctly as possible the content of the faith established in the Bible, we could say: the Lord has started a love story with us and wants to sum up all creation in it. Ultimately, the antidote to the evil that threatens us and the whole world can only be that we abandon ourselves to this love. This is the real antidote to evil. The power of evil arises from our refusal to love God. Anyone who entrusts himself to the love of God is redeemed. Our not being redeemed is a consequence of our inability to love God. Learning to love God is therefore the path of redemption for man.

Now if we try to explain a little more fully this essential content of God's revelation, we could say: the first fundamental gift that faith offers us is the certainty that God exists. A world without God can be nothing but a world without meaning. Indeed, where does everything that exists come from? In any case, it would have no spiritual foundation. It would somehow exist, and that is all, and it would be devoid of any purpose and meaning. Then there would no longer be any criteria of good or evil. Therefore might would make right, and nothing else. Power then becomes the only principle. Truth does not matter; in reality, it does not even exist. Only if things have a spiritual foundation, only if things are willed and thought out—only if there is a Creator God who is good and wills the good—can the life of man have meaning, too.

The existence of God as Creator and measure of all things is first and foremost a primordial requirement. But a God who did not manifest himself at all, who did not make himself known, would remain a conjecture and therefore could not determine the shape of our life. For God to be really God in this deliberate creation, we must expect that he will manifest himself in some form. He has done so in many ways, and he did it decisively in the call that was addressed to Abraham, giving to mankind, in its search for God, the orientation that surpasses all expectation: God himself becomes a creature. He speaks as a man with us humans.

Thus the sentence "God is" finally becomes truly glad tidings, precisely because it is more than knowledge, because it generates love and is love. Making people aware of this again is the first and fundamental task that the Lord assigns to us.

A society in which God is absent, a society that no longer knows him and treats him as if he did not exist, is a society that loses its standards. Our era coined the catchphrase "the death of God". When God dies in a society—we were assured—it becomes free. In reality, the death of God in a society also signifies the end of its freedom, because the meaning that provides its orientation dies—and because the standards disappear that once pointed us in the right direction by teaching us to distinguish good from evil. Western society is a society in which God is absent in the public sphere because he supposedly no longer has anything to say about it. And therefore it is a society in which the standards and the measure of what is human are increasingly lost. In some matters, then, it suddenly becomes noticeable that what is evil and destroys man has become quite commonplace. So it is with pedophilia. Theoretically considered not too long ago as fully legitimate, it spread more and more. And now we are shocked and scandalized to realize that crimes are committed against our children and young people that threaten to destroy them. The fact that this could spread even in the Church and among priests should especially shock and scandalize us.

How could pedophilia reach such proportions? In the final analysis, the reason lies in the absence of God. Even we Christians and priests prefer not to talk about God, because this kind of talk seems to have no practical usefulness. After the upheavals of World War II, we in Germany had framed our constitution, explicitly declaring ourselves responsible before God, as a guiding principle. Half a century later, it was no longer possible, in the European Constitution, to include responsibility before God as a standard. God is seen as the concern of a small special interest group, and he can no longer be taken as a standard for the community as a whole. This decision reflects the situation in the West, where God has become the private affair of a minority.

The paramount task that must ensue from the moral confusion of our time is for us personally to begin again to live by God, turning to him and obedient to him. Above all, we ourselves must learn again to acknowledge God as the foundation of our life instead of leaving him aside as though he were some empty cliché. I still remember the warning that the great theologian Hans Urs von Balthasar once wrote to me on one of his calling cards. "The triune God, Father, Son, and Holy Spirit—do not presuppose him, but propose him!" Indeed, even in theology, God is often presupposed as a matter of course, without dealing with him concretely. The subject "God" seems so unreal, so far removed from the things that concern us. And yet, everything changes if God is not presupposed but proposed, if we do not leave him somehow in the background but acknowledge him as the center of our thoughts, words, and actions.

God became man for us. Man, his creature, is so close to his heart that he united himself with him, concretely entering history. He speaks with us, lives with us, suffers with us, and took death upon himself for us. Of course we talk about this in theology at great length with scholarly words and concepts. But this is precisely how the danger arises of us making ourselves masters of the faith instead of letting ourselves be renewed and mastered by the faith.

Let us reflect on this with regard to one central issue, the celebration of the Holy Eucharist. Our relationship with the Eucharist can only cause concern. The Second Vatican Council correctly intended to place once again

at the center of Christian life and of the Church's very
existence this sacrament of the Presence of the Body and
Blood of Christ, of the Presence of his Person, of his Passion, death, and Resurrection. To some extent, this really
has happened, and we should be grateful to the Lord for it.

And yet a different attitude is widely predominant: not
a new reverence for the presence of Christ's death and
Resurrection, but a way of dealing with him that destroys
the greatness of the Mystery. Declining participation in the
Sunday celebration of the Eucharist shows how little we
Christians of today are capable of appreciating the greatness of this gift, which consists in his Real Presence. The
Eucharist is degraded to a mere ceremonial gesture when
it is considered self-evident that good manners require
that it be distributed to all the relatives and friends who are
invited to family celebrations or on occasions such as wed-
dings and funerals. In some places, as a matter of course,
those who attend receive the Most Blessed Sacrament simply because they are there; this shows that Communion is
now viewed merely as a ceremonial gesture. If we reflect
on what should be done, it is clear that we do not need
another Church of our own design. Rather, what is necessary is a renewal of faith in the reality of Jesus Christ given
to us in the Blessed Sacrament.

In conversations with victims of pedophilia, I have
become more and more acutely aware of this necessity.
A young woman who used to serve as an altar girl told
me that the assistant pastor—who was her superior, given
that she was an altar girl—always introduced the sexual
abuse he committed against her with the words: "This is
my body which is given for you." Obviously this woman
can no longer hear the words of the Consecration without
reexperiencing all the terrible suffering of the abuse that
she endured. Yes, we must urgently implore the Lord for

forgiveness, and above all else we must beg him and ask him to teach us all to understand again the magnitude of his Passion, of his sacrifice. And we must do all we can to protect the gift of the Holy Eucharist from abuse.

Finally, there is the mystery of the Church. Still engraved on my memory are the words with which Romano Guardini, almost one hundred years ago now, expressed the joyful hope that was asserting itself then in him and in many others: "An event of inestimable importance has begun; the Church is awakening in souls." By this he meant that the Church was no longer, as in the past, merely an apparatus presented to us from outside and experienced and perceived as a kind of authority. Rather, in his view, it was starting to be perceived as alive in people's hearts—as something that is not just external but touches us interiorly. About half a century later, reflecting again on this process and looking at what had just happened, I was tempted to turn the sentence upside down: "The Church is dying in souls." Indeed, the Church today is widely viewed as just some kind of political apparatus. In fact, people speak of her almost exclusively in terms of political categories, and this is true even for some bishops who to a great extent formulate their idea of the Church of tomorrow in exclusively political terms. The crisis caused by the many cases of clerical abuse drives us to regard the Church as a failure, which we must now decisively take into our own hands and redesign from the ground up. However, a Church that we build can offer no hope.

Jesus himself compared the Church to a fishing net in which there are good and bad fish, since God himself is the one who will ultimately have to separate them. There is also the parable of the Church as a field in which grows the good grain that God himself sowed, but also the weeds

that an "enemy" stealthily sowed in it. Indeed, the weeds
in God's field, the Church, are so plentiful as to be con-
spicuous, and the bad fish in the net likewise show their
strength. Nevertheless, the field is still God's field, and the
net remains God's fishing net. In every age, there are and
there will be not only the weeds and the bad fish, but also
God's sowing and the good fish. Forcefully proclaiming
both proportionately is not false apologetics, but a necessary service to the truth.

In this matter, it is necessary to refer to an important passage in the Revelation of Saint John where the
devil is called the "accuser" who day and night accuses
our brethren before God (Rev 12:10). In this way, the
Book of Revelation repeats an idea that is central to
the frame story in the Book of Job (Job 1; 2:1–10;
42:7–16). It relates that the devil tries to discredit Job's
righteousness and integrity as being purely external and
superficial. This is exactly what the Book of Revelation
is speaking about: the devil wants to prove that there are
no righteous men, that all human righteousness is just an
outward display, and that if he could test it more, the
appearance of righteousness would quickly vanish. The
narrative begins with a dispute between God and the devil
in which God refers to Job as a truly righteous man. Now
Job will therefore be put to the test, to determine who is
right. "Take away his possessions," the devil argues, "and
you will see that none of his piety remains." God allows
him to make this attempt, and Job passes this test. Then
the devil goes on to say: "Skin for skin! All that a man has
he will give for his life. But put forth your hand now, and
touch his bone and his flesh, and he will curse you to your
face" (Job 2:4–5). And so God grants the devil a second
chance. He is allowed to touch Job's skin as well. The
only thing he may not do is kill the man. For Christians, it

is clear that this Job who stands before God as an exemplar of all mankind is Jesus Christ. In the Book of Revelation, the drama of humanity is presented in all its breadth. The Creator God is contrasted with the devil, who speaks ill of all creation and all mankind. He addresses not only God but especially men, saying: "Look at what this God has done. On the surface it looks like a good creation, but in reality, as a whole it is disgusting and full of misery." This disparagement of creation is really a disparagement of God. The devil tries to prove that God himself is not good and tries to turn us away from him.

The relevance of what the Book of Revelation tells us here is manifest. Today, the accusation against God focuses above all on discrediting his Church as a whole and thereby turning us away from her. The idea of a better Church of our own creation is really a proposal of the devil, with which he tries to turn us away from the living God by using a deceitful logic that we fall for much too easily. No, even today the Church does not consist only of bad fish and weeds. God's Church still exists today, and even and precisely today she is the instrument by which God saves us. It is very important to contrast the lies and half-truths of the devil with the whole truth: Yes, there is sin in the Church and there is evil. But even today there is also the Holy Church, which is indestructible. Even today there are many people who humbly believe, suffer, and love, in whom the real God, the loving God, manifests himself to us. Even today God has his witnesses (*martyres*) in the world. We have only to be attentive in order to see them and hear them.

The word "martyr" is taken from trial law. In the trial against the devil, Jesus Christ is God's first and authentic witness, the first martyr, whom countless others have followed since then. Today's Church is more than ever a

Church of martyrs and thus a witness to the living God. If we look around with an attentive heart and listen, we can find everywhere today—among uneducated people, but also in the high ranks of the Church—witnesses who testify to God by their life and suffering. Unwillingness to notice them is a symptom of a slothful heart. One of the great essential tasks of our evangelization is, to the best of our ability, to create habitats of faith and above all to find and recognize them.

I live in a house in which a small community continually discovers, in the everyday routine, similar testimonies to the living God and gladly points them out to me. To see and to find the Church alive is a wonderful task that strengthens us, again and again making us glad in our faith.

At the end of my reflections, I would like to thank Pope Francis for everything he is doing to show us, over and over again, the light of God, which even today has not waned. Thank you, Holy Father!

Chapter Six

OCCASIONAL SPEECHES
AND ESSAYS

THE INTERNATIONAL
THEOLOGICAL COMMISSION

To the International Theological Commission, on the occasion of its fiftieth anniversary, I address my cordial greetings and my special blessing.

The Synod of Bishops and the International Theological Commission as lasting institutions were both given to the Church by Pope Paul VI in order to make lasting and continue the experiences of Vatican Council II. The separation that had been manifested at the council between the theology that was developing throughout the world and the papal Magisterium had to be overcome. As far back as the beginning of the twentieth century, the Pontifical Biblical Commission had been established, which, however, in its original form was itself part of the papal Magisterium, whereas after Vatican II it was transformed into an organ for theological consultation at the service of the Magisterium, so as to provide a competent opinion in biblical matters. According to the arrangement established by Paul VI, the prefect of the Congregation for the Doctrine of the Faith is at the same time president of the Pontifical Biblical Commission and of the International Theological Commission, which, however, select their respective secretaries in-house.

Welcome speech of Pope Emeritus Benedict XVI to mark the fiftieth anniversary of the institution of the International Theological Commission, Mater Ecclesiae Monastery, October 22, 2019. The document was published on the website of the International Theological Commission under the heading "Pontifical Speeches".

The purpose was to make clear in this way that neither commission is an organ of the Congregation for the Doctrine of the Faith, which might have dissuaded some theologians from agreeing to become members of them. Franjo Cardinal Šeper compared the relation between the prefect of the Congregation for the Doctrine of the Faith and the presidency of the two commissions to the structure of the Austro-Hungarian monarchy: the emperor of Austria and the king of Hungary were the same person, while the two countries lived autonomously alongside each other. Nevertheless, the Congregation for the Doctrine of the Faith places its practical resources at the disposal of the sessions of the commission and of those who participate in them, and for this purpose it created the post of the technical secretary, who from time to time provides the necessary assistance.

No doubt the expectations associated with the newly constituted International Theological Commission were at first greater than what could then be accomplished over the course of a half-century of history. The first period of sessions of the commission produced a study, *Le Ministère sacerdotal* [Priestly ministry] (October 10, 1970), which was published in 1971 by the Cerf publishing house in Paris; it was intended as background material for the first major gathering of the Synod of Bishops. For the synod itself, the Theological Commission appointed a specific group of theologians who, as consultors, were available during the first session of the Synod of Bishops and, thanks to their extraordinary work, made it possible for the synod to publish immediately a document on the priesthood drawn up by the synod itself. Since then, this has not happened again. Very soon, instead, the genre of the post-synodal exhortation developed, which of course is not a document of the synod but a papal Magisterial document that takes up again as broadly as possible the statements of the synod and does this in such a way that the worldwide episcopate still speaks together with the pope.[1]

Personally, I recall in a particularly vivid way the first five-year term of the International Theological Commission. The basic orientation of the commission and its essential method of working had to be defined, thus establishing in the final analysis the direction in which Vatican II was to be interpreted.

Besides the major figures of the council—Henri de Lubac, Yves Congar, Karl Rahner, Jorge Medina Estévez, Philippe Delhaye, Gérard Philips, Carlo Colombo of Milan, who was considered the personal theologian of Paul VI, and Father Cipriano Vagaggini—important theologians belonged to the commission who oddly enough had not found a place at the council.

Among them, besides Hans Urs von Balthasar, we should mention above all Louis Bouyer. A convert and a monk, he had an extremely stubborn personality, and his careless candor displeased a number of bishops. He was, however, a great collaborator with an incredible breadth

---

[1] The document on the diaconate published in 2003 was in a certain way an exception; it was drawn up at the request of the Congregation for the Doctrine of the Faith and was supposed to provide an orientation with regard to the question of the diaconate, particularly with regard to the question of whether this sacramental ministry could be conferred on women, also. The document, drafted with great care, did not arrive at an unequivocal conclusion with regard to a possible diaconate for women. It was decided to submit the question to the patriarchs of the Eastern churches. Of them, however, only a very few responded. It is evident that the question itself was as such difficult to understand for the tradition of the Eastern church. And so this wide-ranging study concluded with the statement that the purely historical perspective did not make it possible to arrive at any definitive certainty. In the final analysis, the question had to be decided on the doctrinal level. Cf. Commissione Teologica Internazionale, *Documenti 1969–2004*, 2nd ed. (Bologna: Edizioni Studio Domenicano, 2010), 651–766.

of knowledge. Then Father Marie-Joseph Le Guillou came on the scene, especially during the Synod of Bishops; he worked entire nights, thus substantially making possible the document of the synod. Unfortunately, though, with such a radical way of serving, he contracted Parkinson's disease, and thus took his leave too quickly from this life and from his theological work. Rudolf Schnackenburg embodied German exegesis with all the ambition that characterized it. Then André Feuillet and also Heinz Schürmann of Erfurt gladly became involved as a sort of opposite pole. Their exegesis was of a more spiritual style. Finally, I must also mention Professor Johannes Feiner of Coira, who, as a representative of the Pontifical Council for Unity, played a particular role on the commission. The question of whether the Catholic Church should join the World Council of Churches in Geneva as a regular, full-fledged member became a decisive point concerning the direction that the Church should take in the postconciliar era. After a dramatic confrontation over the question, it was finally decided in the negative, which prompted Feiner and Rahner to leave the commission.

In the second five-year term, new figures made their appearance on the Theological Commission: two young Italians, Carlo Caffarra and Father Raniero Cantalamessa, conferred new importance on theology in the Italian language. In addition to the members already present, German-language theology was strengthened thanks to Father Otto Semmelroth, a Jesuit conciliar theologian whose ability to draft documents quickly for various needs proved as useful to the commission as it had been during the council. Together with him and with Karl Lehmann, a new generation stepped into the limelight whose concept started to be asserted clearly in the documents now being produced.

Yet my intention is not to continue with the presentation of the notable figures who worked on the Theological Commission, but rather to offer some reflections on the topics that were selected. At first it addressed questions concerning the relation between Magisterium and theology, on which it is always necessary to reflect continually. What the commission said on this topic over the course of the last half-century deserves another hearing and further meditation.

Under the guidance of Lehmann, the fundamental question of *Gaudium et spes* was also analyzed—that is, the problem of human progress and Christian salvation. Another topic that inevitably emerged in this area was liberation theology, which at that time was by no means only a theoretical problem but also determined the life of the Church in South America in a very concrete way and threatened it. The passion that animated those theologians matched the pragmatic and even political importance of the question.[2]

Besides the questions regarding the relation between the Magisterium of the Church and the teaching of theology, one of the main areas of the work of the Theological Commission was always the problem of moral theology. Perhaps it is significant that at the beginning there was no voice of representatives of moral theology, but only experts in exegesis and dogmatic theology. In 1974, Heinz Schürmann and Hans Urs von Balthasar started the discussion with their theses, which then continued in 1977 with the debate

---

[2] Allow me to note here a little personal recollection. My friend Father Juan Alfaro, S.J., who at the Gregorian taught primarily on the doctrine of grace, for reasons that are totally incomprehensible to me had become over the years an impassioned supporter of liberation theology. I did not want to lose my friendship with him and so that was the one time in the entire period of my membership on the commission that I skipped the general assembly.

on the sacrament of matrimony. The opposition between the sides and the lack of a common basic orientation, from which we still suffer today as much as then, became clear to me at that moment in a dramatic way: on the one hand was the American moral theologian Professor William May, the father of many children, who always came to visit us with his wife and defended the most rigorous traditional concept. Twice he had to experience the unanimous rejection of his proposal, something that never had happened otherwise. He burst into tears, and I myself could not manage to console him. A position close to his, as I recall, was adopted by Professor John Finnis, who taught in the United States and expressed the same approach and the same concept in a new way. He was indeed taken seriously from the theological perspective, yet he did not succeed either in reaching any consensus. In the fifth five-year term, a member of the school of Professor Tadeusz Styczeń—the friend of Pope John Paul II—joined the commission: Professor Andrzej Szostek, an intelligent and promising advocate of the classic position. He in turn did not succeed in creating a consensus. Finally, Father Servais Pinckaers tried to develop in Thomistic terms an ethic of virtues that appeared to me very reasonable and convincing, and yet it too did not succeed in reaching a consensus.

The difficulty of the situation can also be gathered from the fact that John Paul II, who had moral theology particularly at heart, ultimately decided to postpone the final revision of his moral encyclical *Veritatis splendor*, intending to wait first of all for the *Catechism of the Catholic Church*. He did not publish his encyclical until August 6, 1993, having again found new coworkers for the project. I think that the Theological Commission must continue to keep the problem in mind and must fundamentally continue in the effort to search for a consensus.

Lastly I would like to highlight another aspect of the commission's work. In its sessions, the voice of the young Churches, too, made itself heard more and more and ever more loudly with regard to the following question: To what extent are they bound to the Western tradition, and to what extent can other cultures establish a new theological culture? Above all, the theologians from Africa, on the one hand, and from India, on the other, were the ones to raise the question, although to date it has not been possible to address it thematically. Similarly, until now the theme of dialogue with the other major world religions has not been taken up.[3]

Finally, notwithstanding all the inadequacies inherent in human seeking and inquiry, we must express a word of sincere gratitude. The International Theological Commission, despite all the efforts, has not been able to achieve a moral unity of theology and of theologians in the world. Anyone who was waiting for this was harboring wrong expectations about the possibilities of such a work. And yet even so, the commission's voice has become a voice that is listened to and that, in some way, indicates the basic orientation that a serious theological effort must follow at this historical moment. To our gratitude for what has been accomplished in a half a century we add the hope for further fruitful work, in which the one faith can lead also to a common orientation of thinking and speaking about God and his revelation.

---

[3] I would like to point out again here a curious particular case. A Japanese Jesuit, Father Shun'ichi Takayanagi, had become so familiar with the thought of the German Lutheran theologian Gerhard Ebeling that he argued completely on the basis of his thought and language. But no one on the Theological Commission was well enough acquainted with Ebeling to allow a fruitful dialogue to develop, so that the erudite Japanese Jesuit left the commission because his language and his thought failed to find any place in it.

As for me personally, working on the International Theological Commission gave me the joy of encountering other languages and other forms of thought. Above all, though, it was for me a continual occasion for humility, which sees the limits of what is our own and thus opens the path to the greater truth.

Only humility can find the truth, and truth in turn is the foundation of love, on which everything ultimately depends.

ONE HUNDRED YEARS SINCE THE BIRTH OF SAINT JOHN PAUL II

On May 18, we will celebrate the centenary of the birth of Pope John Paul II in the little Polish town of Wadowice.

Poland, which had been divided and occupied by the three neighboring empires—Prussia, Russia, and Austria—for more than a century, regained its independence after World War I. It was an event that raised great hopes but also demanded great efforts, given that the reviving state constantly felt the pressure of both the major powers, Germany and Russia. In this situation of oppression, but above all of hope, the young Karol Wojtyła grew up; unfortunately he very soon lost his mother, his brother, and finally his father, to whom he owed his profound and fervent devotion. Young Karol's particular attraction to literature and the theater led him to study these subjects after earning a secondary school diploma.

In order to avoid being deported to Germany for forced labor, in the autumn of 1940 he started to work as a laborer in the quarry that belonged to the chemical factory Solvay.[4] In the autumn of 1942, he made the definitive decision to enter the seminary of Kraków, which had been organized secretly by the archbishop of Kraków, Adam Sapieha, in his diocese. While still a laborer, he started to study theology from old textbooks, so that he was able to be ordained a

---

The text was written on May 4, 2010, in anticipation of the one hundredth anniversary of the birth of Saint John Paul II, which fell on May 18, 2020.

[4] John Paul II, *Gift and Mystery* (New York: Doubleday, 1996).

priest on November 1, 1946. However, he learned theology not only from books, but also by drawing useful lessons from the specific context in which he and his country found themselves. This would become a distinctive trait that would characterize him throughout his life and activity. He learned from books, but he also assimilated the lived experience of current issues that tormented him. Thus, for him as a young bishop—an auxiliary bishop since 1958 and from 1964 on archbishop of Kraków—Vatican Council II was the school of his whole life and of his work. The important questions that emerged, especially regarding the so-called Schema XIII—later the Constitution *Gaudium et spes*—were his personal questions. The answers worked out at the council showed the direction that his work would take, first as a bishop and then as pope.

On October 16, 1978, when Cardinal Wojtyła was elected the successor of Peter, the Church was in a dramatic situation. The deliberations of the council were presented in public as a dispute about the faith itself, which thus seemed to lack its character of infallible and inviolable certainty. For example, a Bavarian pastor described the situation in the following words: "In the end we fell into a mistaken faith." This sense that nothing was certain anymore, that everything could be up for debate, was further heightened by the way in which the liturgical reform was conducted. In the end, it seemed that even in the liturgy anything goes. Paul VI conducted the council vigorously and decisively until its conclusion, after which he confronted increasingly difficult problems, which finally called the Church herself into question. The sociologists of that time compared the situation of the Church to that of the Soviet Union under Gorbachev, where in the search for necessary reforms, the entire powerful image of the Soviet state finally collapsed.

And so the new pope was confronted in fact with a task that would be quite difficult to face with human abilities alone. From the start, however, John Paul II exhibited the ability to awaken a renewed admiration for Christ and for his Church. In the beginning were the words that he proclaimed at the outset of his pontificate, his battle cry: "Be not afraid! Open, open wide the doors to Christ!" This tone characterized his whole pontificate, making him a renovator and liberator of the Church. This was because the new pope came from a country where the council had been received in a positive way. The decisive factor was not doubting everything, but rather renewing everything with joy.

On the 104 major pastoral journeys that the pontiff made throughout the world, he preached the Gospel as glad tidings, thus also explaining the duty to accept what is good and to welcome Christ.

In fourteen encyclicals, he presented in a new way the faith of the Church and her human teaching. Inevitably, then, he provoked opposition in the doubt-filled churches of the West.

Today it seems to me important to point out the real core from which we should read the message contained in his various documents, which came to the attention of us all at the hour of his death. Pope John Paul II died in the first hours of the Feast of the Divine Mercy, which he himself had instituted. I would like to add initially here a little personal note that shows something that is important for understanding the essence and the conduct of this pope. From the start, John Paul II was very impressed by the message of the nun from Kraków, Faustina Kowalska, who had presented the mercy of God as the essential core of the whole Christian faith and had tried to institute the Feast of the Divine Mercy. After consultations, the pope assigned the Sunday after Easter (*Dominica in albis*) as the liturgical day for it. However, before making a definitive decision, he asked the opinion of the Congregation of the Doctrine of the Faith in order to weigh the suitability of that choice. We gave a negative response, maintaining that such an important, ancient, and meaningful day as *Dominica in albis* should not be encumbered with new ideas. For the Holy Father, accepting our "no" was certainly not easy. But he did so with all humility and accepted our second "no". Finally, he formulated a proposal that, while leaving the Sunday after Easter with its historical significance, allowed him to introduce the Divine Mercy into its original meaning. There were often cases in which I was impressed by the humility of that great pope, who renounced his favorite ideas when the official organizations—from whom these things traditionally had to be requested—did not give their consent.

When John Paul II breathed his last in this world, it was already after Evening Prayer I of the Feast of the Divine Mercy. This illuminated the hour of his death: the light of God's mercy shone on his death as a comforting message. In his last book, *Memory and Identity*, which appeared almost on the vigil of his death, the pope presented briefly once again the message of the Divine Mercy. In it he pointed out that Sister Faustina died before the horrors of World War II, but had already spread the Lord's response to those horrors. "Evil does not have the last word! The Paschal Mystery confirms that good is ultimately victorious, that life conquers death, and that love triumphs over hate."

The pope's whole life was centered on this determination to accept subjectively as his own the objective core of the Christian faith—the teaching of salvation—and to allow others to accept it. Thanks to the Risen Christ, the mercy of God is for everyone. Even though this core of Christian existence is given to us only in faith, it also has a philosophical significance, because—since the Divine Mercy is not a matter of empirical fact—we must also take into account a world in which the final counterbalance between good and evil is unrecognizable. Ultimately, beyond this objective historical meaning, it is indispensable for everyone to know that the mercy of God in the end will prove to be stronger than our weakness. Here we must find the interior unity between the message of John Paul II and the fundamental intentions of Pope Francis: contrary to what is often said, John Paul II was not a rigorist in his teaching about morality. By demonstrating the essential importance of the Divine Mercy, he gives us the opportunity to accept the moral demands that are made on man, although we cannot satisfy them fully. Our moral efforts are undertaken in the light of God's mercy, which is revealed as a force that heals our weakness.

As John Paul II lay dying, Saint Peter's Square was full of people, especially young people, who wanted to encounter their pope for the last time. I will never forget the moment in which Archbishop Leonardo Sandri announced the pope's death. Above all I will not forget the moment when the great bell of Saint Peter's revealed this news. On the day of the Holy Father's funeral, you could see many, many banners with the inscription *Santo subito* [A saint immediately]. This was a cry that rose on all sides from the encounter with John Paul II. And there were discussions—not only in Saint Peter's Square, but in various intellectual circles—about the possibility of granting to John Paul II the title of "the Great".

The word "saint" indicates the divine sphere, and the word "great" indicates the human dimension. According to the Church's principles, holiness is evaluated on the basis of two criteria: heroic virtues and miracles. These two criteria are closely interconnected. The concept of "heroic virtues" does not point to an Olympic victory but, rather, to the fact that what is visible in and through a person does not have its source in the man himself, but reveals the action of God in and through him. This is a matter, not of moral competition, but of renouncing one's own greatness. It is about a man who allows God to act within him and, therefore, to make visible through him the action and the power of God.

The same is true for the miracle criterion. Here, too, it is a matter, not of something sensational, but of God's healing goodness becoming visible in a way that surpasses human abilities. A saint is an open man, penetrated by God. A saint is a person open to God, permeated by God. A saint is someone who does not focus his attention on himself, but makes us see and recognize God. The purpose of processes of beatification and canonization is precisely that of testing this to the extent possible according to the norms of the law. As for John Paul II, both processes were conducted rigorously according to the rules in force. And so now he appears before us as a father who shows us the mercy and the goodness of God.

It is more difficult to define correctly the term "great". During the almost two thousand years of the history of the papacy, the title *magnus* was adopted in reference to only two popes: Leo I (440–461) and Gregory I (590–604). The word "great" bears a political stamp in both cases, but in the sense that, through their political successes, something of the mystery of God himself is revealed. Leo the Great, in a conversation with Attila, the leader of the Huns, convinced him to spare Rome, the city of the apostles Peter and Paul. Without arms, without military or political power, he managed to persuade the terrible tyrant to spare

Rome thanks to his own faith conviction. In the struggle of the spirit against power, the spirit proved to be stronger.

Gregory I did not have such a spectacular success, yet he succeeded in saving Rome several times from the Longobards (Lombards)—he too, by opposing temporal power with the spirit, carried off the victory for the spirit.

When we compare the history of both with that of John Paul II, the similarity is undeniable. Like his predecessors, John Paul II had neither a military strength nor political power. In February 1945, during discussions about the future form of Europe and of Germany, someone noted that it was necessary to take account of the pope's opinion, too. Stalin then asked: "How many divisions does the pope have?" Of course he had none. But the power of faith proved to be a force that, at the end of 1989, overthrew the Soviet system of power and made a new beginning possible. There is no doubt that the pope's faith was an important element in smashing that power. And here, too, we can certainly see the greatness that was manifested in the cases of Leo I and Gregory I.

The question of whether or not the title "the Great" will be accepted in this case must be left open. It is true that in John Paul II, the power and the goodness of God became visible to us all. In a moment when the Church is again suffering from the attack of evil, he is for us a sign of hope and consolation.

Dear Saint John Paul II, pray for us!

SEVENTY-FIVE YEARS
SINCE THE DEATH OF
JESUIT FATHER ALFRED DELP

The Feast of Candlemas 2020 marks the seventy-fifth anniversary of the martyrdom of Father Alfred Delp. It is important, or, rather, it is necessary to revive the memory of this great witness to Jesus Christ in dark times. We are all too much infected, indeed, by a mentality that makes us deaf, blind, and mute with regard to the Lord's message and conforms us instead to this world.

I am fortunate that my first assignment as assistant priest was in the very same parish in which Father Delp had lived, too. To that same parish belonged one of my pre-decessors as assistant priest, the Reverend Doctor Josef Wehrle, who was executed for the same reasons as Father Delp. Later on the parish had been moved a bit more to the east and found its new headquarters in the Church of the Most Precious Blood, built by the famous archi-tect Hans Döllgast. But the old Baroque Church of Saint George, near which Father Delp lived, continued to depend on that parish and became increasingly important especially for Catholic youth. Every week, at six in the morning, we used to celebrate Holy Mass together with a considerable crowd of young people. Meanwhile the local

February 2, 2020, the Feast of Candlemas (Presentation of our Lord), was the seventy-fifth anniversary of the death of Jesuit Father Alfred Delp. On October 15, 2019, Pope Benedict wrote this text for the occasion. Not previously pub-lished in Italian or English.

cemetery belonging to the Church of Saint George had been reserved for the eminent inhabitants of the city of Munich who had the means of getting buried there. And the Catholic youth had turned the mortuary into a sort of youth center in which I spent many evenings together with the young people. Father Max Blumschein, initially pastor of Saint George parish and then, after it was relocated, of Most Precious Blood, went back to live in Saint George after his retirement and died there while bringing extreme unction to a parishioner.

Father Delp's activity did not hinge on the parish, but he lived there anyway and was arrested one morning at the end of the Holy Mass that he celebrated in Saint George Church. All this moved us profoundly then. Today, though, there is a great risk of forgetting, and it is important to combat this danger.

At first, Father Alfred Delp had belonged to the "Kreisau Circle" simply as an expert on the social teaching of the Church and as a person inspired by the question of the right order of human affairs; and this was precisely how he matured little by little in his resistance to Hitler and his dictatorship. What he wrote from his cell with his hands in chains struck us profoundly in the aftermath of the war. But someone who reads today what he wrote then is again touched by the light of Christ, which made this man mature more and more by making him a great witness to true life.

Father Franz von Tattenbach, in whose hands Father Delp took his final vows in prison, was our spiritual father at [the major seminary in] Freising. He did not make great speeches about what had happened, but neither did he keep hidden what had impressed him so deeply.

Father Delp certainly could be killed in the body by the executioners of that time, just as his hands could be chained, but the Word of God is not chained and speaks to us again and again precisely through the bloody testimony of the martyrs. May the Lord help us, in our time and in the way that we ask, to be witnesses to Jesus Christ once again.

"HIS SILENCE IS ALSO HIS WAY OF EXPRESSING HIMSELF"

Interview on Saint Joseph

Your Holiness, Scripture does not record a single word spoken by Saint Joseph. Is there however, in your opinion, a statement in the New Testament that expresses the saint's character in a particularly suitable way?

It is true, no words of Saint Joseph are handed down to us by the New Testament within his story. But there is a correspondence between the task entrusted to Saint Joseph by the angel who appears to him in a dream and his action, a correspondence that clearly characterizes him. In the episode of the command that he receives in a dream to take Mary as his spouse, his response is given in a simple sentence: "When Joseph woke from sleep, he did as the angel of the Lord commanded him" (Mt 1:24). The correspondence between the task and the action is manifested even more strikingly in the episode of the flight into Egypt, in which the same words [in Greek] are used: "He rose and took the child and his mother" (Mt 2:14). Both expressions are used again a third time at the news of Herod's

An interview with Reina Einig in *Die Tagespost*. "Sein Schweigen ist zugleich sein Wort", *Die Tagespost*, April 1, 2021, 33–34. An English translation was published by the *National Catholic Register* on the same day. The English text here was translated from the Italian edition of *What Is Christianity?*

death and of the possibility of returning to the Holy Land. The words that characterize Joseph follow, one after the other: "He rose and took the child and his mother" (Mt 2:21). The nocturnal warning about the danger of Archelaus does not have the same authority as the preceding information. Saint Joseph's action in response says much more simply: "Being warned in a dream he withdrew to the district of Galilee" (Mt 2:22). The same basic attitude is manifested finally, in an altogether different way, in the episode of the adoration of the Magi who came from the East: "Going into the house they saw the child with Mary his mother" (Mt 2:11). Saint Joseph does not appear in the meeting between the Magi and the Child Jesus. This silent reluctance to appear is also characteristic and shows very clearly that along with the formation of the Holy Family, he took upon himself a service that required great decision-making and organizational ability, but together with a great capacity for self-denial. His silence is at the same time his message. It expresses his "yes" to what he took upon himself in binding himself to Mary and to Jesus.

What impressions do you have from your pilgrimages in the Holy Land that are particularly connected with the life of your patron saint?

I must say that during the visits that I made to the Holy Land, Saint Joseph almost never appeared. It is natural that he should not be mentioned at the major sites of the public ministry of Jesus in Galilee, especially near the Lake of Gennesaret and the surrounding areas, as well as in Judea. It would contradict his fundamental attitude of obedient silence and his being in second place. However, one could certainly expect a word about him in Nazareth as well as in Bethlehem. Nazareth, in particular, refers to the figure of

Joseph. Indeed, it is a place that, outside of the New Testament, is not mentioned anywhere else in written sources. The total absence of written testimonies on Nazareth outside of the New Testament is so striking that Pierre Benoit, one of the most important exegetes, who for a long time headed the École Biblique of the Dominicans in the Holy Land, once told me personally that he had finally come to the conclusion that Nazareth had never existed. But, before he made this apparent finding public, news arrived just in time about the success in Nazareth of the excavations that restored this site to us. The head of the group of Franciscan archeologists, for his part, admitted that, after long efforts in vain to find traces of ancient Nazareth, he had been almost on the point of abandoning the whole effort. He was all the more glad, therefore, when he brought to light the first traces and finally the entire site.

Indeed, for Matthew—who puts an Old Testament passage at the basis of every event in the life of Jesus as an attempt to demonstrate that Jesus truly was the Messiah foretold by the Old Testament—the fact that there was no prophetic prediction that had spoken in some way about Nazareth presented a difficulty. This was a fundamental difficulty for the legitimization of Jesus as the promised Messiah: Nazareth in itself obtained no promise (cf. Jn 1:46). And, nevertheless, Matthew found three ways to legitimize Jesus the Nazarene as Messiah, too. The messianic trilogy by Isaiah in chapters 7, 9, and 11 relates in chapter 9 the prophecy whereby a light will shine in a land of darkness. Matthew identifies the land of darkness with semi-pagan Galilee where Jesus began his journey.

A second legitimization of Nazareth is obtained, for Matthew, from the inscription over the Cross composed by the pagan Pilate, in which he deliberately proposes the "title" (which means the legal motivation) for the crucifixion: "Jesus of Nazareth, the King of the Jews" (Jn 19:19). This term has been handed down in two forms—Nazarene and Nazirite—which certainly refers, on the one hand, to Jesus' total consecration to God, but recalls, on the other hand, his geographical origin. Thus Nazareth, as part of the mystery of Jesus through the pagan Pilate, is inseparably connected with the figure of Jesus himself.

Finally it occurs to me that a catechesis on Saint Joseph given in the Holy Land could also recall a third aspect that summarizes and adds greater depth to the two preceding ones. In a one of the best-known and beautiful German Christmas carols, we see Jesus as a little rose (*Röslein*) given to us by the Virgin Mary in that Holy Night. In the text currently in use, it speaks at first about a "rose" (*Ros*), then, in the second stanza, Mary is called the "little rose" (*Röslein*) about which Isaiah spoke and is pointed out as the Virgin and Mother who bore the little flower for us. The text, therefore, presents several shifts that need some explanation. My personal hypothesis is that originally the word was not *Ros* but *Reis*, that is, shoot or sprout; and so this brings us straight to the words of the prophet, which read: "There shall come forth a shoot from the stump of Jesse" (Is 11:1).

The stump of Jesse, who was the forefather of the dynasty of David, which had received the promise of lasting forever, refers to the contradiction between promise and reality that was intolerable for a believing Israelite: the Davidic dynasty disappeared, and only a dead stump remained. But that very same dead stump now becomes a sign of hope: from it a shoot unexpectedly sprouts once again. This paradox, in the genealogy of Jesus in Matthew 1:1–17 and Luke 3:23–38, is recorded in the form of a present reality and for the evangelist conceals within it a tacit reference to the birth of Jesus from the Virgin Mary.

Joseph is not the true biological father of Jesus, but he is so legally, by the Law that is constitutive for Israel. The mystery of the shoot becomes still deeper here. The stump of Jesse, by itself, no longer generates life; the stump is truly dead. And yet it bears new life in the son of the Virgin Mary, whose legal father is Joseph.

All this has to do with the theme of Nazareth, inasmuch as the word Nazareth seems to contain within it the term *nezer, naser* (shoot). The name Nazareth could also be translated as "village of the shoot". A German researcher who spent his life in Israel even speculated that Nazareth was born as a settlement for Davidites after the Babylonian Exile and that this had been indicated obscurely in the name Nazareth. In any case, the mystery of Saint Joseph is profoundly related to the locality of Nazareth. He is the one who, as a shoot from the root of Jesse, expresses the hope of Israel.

Saint Joseph is traditionally invoked as patron saint of a happy death. What do you think about this custom?

We can say with certainty that Saint Joseph died during the time of Jesus' hidden life. He is mentioned one last time in Luke 4:22 after the first public visit of Jesus to the synagogue in Nazareth. The amazement of the crowd at what Jesus says and how he says it turns into perplexity, and they ask each other: "Is this not the son of Joseph?" The fact that subsequently he is no longer mentioned, while it is his mother and his "brothers" who ask to see Jesus, is a certain sign that he was no longer alive. Therefore, the idea that Saint Joseph concluded his earthly life in Mary's care is well founded. Praying to him to accompany us kindly, too, in our final hour is therefore an absolutely warranted form of piety.

How was your patron saint's day celebrated in your family?

Saint Joseph's Day was my father's patronal feast and mine, and, within the practical limitations, it was celebrated properly. Most times my mother, with her savings, somehow managed to buy an important book (for example, *Der kleine Herder* [a small reference book]). Then there was a table-cloth specifically for the feast day, which made the breakfast festive. We would drink fresh-ground coffee, which my father liked very much, although usually we could not afford it. Finally on the table there was always a primrose as a sign of spring, which Saint Joseph brings with him. And to top it off, Mother would bake a cake with icing, which completely expressed the extraordinary character of the feast. In this way, the special quality of the Feast of Saint Joseph was tangible from early morning on.

Have you experienced personally in your life the intercession of your patron saint?

When I notice that a prayer has been answered, I do not trace the cause of it back to individual intercessions, but feel indebted to them as a whole.

Pope Francis announced the Year of Saint Joseph, reminding the faithful that Saint Joseph was declared the patron of the Universal Church in 1870. What hope do you place in this gesture?

I am particularly glad, of course, that Pope Francis has re-awakened among the faithful an awareness of Saint Joseph's importance; and therefore I read with enormous gratitude and most sincere agreement the Apostolic Letter *Patris corde* that the Holy Father wrote for the 150th anniversary of the proclamation of Saint Joseph as patron of the Universal

Church. It is a very simple text that comes from the heart and is addressed to the heart, and for precisely this reason, it is very profound. I think that this document should be read diligently and meditated on by the faithful; it would thus contribute to the purification and deepening of our veneration of the saints in general and of Saint Joseph in particular.